CW00971803

EUROPEAN STAM. ~~DESIGN~~

A Semiotic Approach To Designing Messages

EUROPEAN STAMP DESIGN

A Semiotic Approach To Designing Messages

DAVID SCOTT

A.D. ACADEMY EDITIONS

ACKNOWLEDGEMENTS

For Michael and Sylvia Goaman

A great many people have assisted me in the preparation of this book. I wish first to thank the artists Robert Ballagh, Hans Erni and his wife Doris, and Michael and Sylvia Goaman for their invaluable assistance and for permission to reproduce their work; the last two also for their generous hospitality; my publishers, especially my editor Nicola Kearton, whose faith in the project led to Academy Editions taking it on, and Andrea Bettella, design co-ordinator at Academy; John Harley for admitting me to the stamp archives at Harrisons, who funded the associated European Stamp exhibition at the Design Museum, London, and permitted the reproduction of two unperforated sheets by Edmund Dulac; the British Post Office, in particular Mr John Ryan, for kindly allowing the reproduction in colour, actual size, of the British stamps illustrated in plates I-X; The Crown Agents Stamp Bureau for kindly permitting the reproduction of the British Commonwealth stamps on plates XXX-XXXVIII; Douglas Muir, curator, Philately, at the National Postal Museum, for his assistance and for permission to reproduce the Arnold Machin portrait bust of HRH Queen Elizabeth II and the 1935 Dulac Jubilee artwork; Mr Jean-Louis Grandveau, Technical Advisor at the Ministry of Posts and Telecommunications in Paris, for kindly permitting reproduction of the French stamps in Plates XI-XV; the Réunion des Musées Nationaux for permission to reproduce Eugène Delacroix's *La Liberté aux Barricades* of 1830; Le Musée de la Révolution Française à Vizille for permission to reproduce Nanine Vallain's *La Liberté* of 1793; at the Swiss PTT, Mr Peter Meier, Director of the PTT (Stamps Section) for his invaluable assistance in many matters and for permitting the reproduction of material in the Swiss National Postal Museum, Bern, and Mr Marc Imobersteg, director of the PTT Library, for his help with bibliography; Pro Helvetia, for funding a ten-day visit to Switzerland to research Swiss stamps in May 1994, and in particular, Ms Denise Pelozzi, for helping to arrange such a successful programme of visits; Dr Hans Lüthy for admitting me to the library facilities of the Swiss Institute for Art Research, Zürich; Professor Stanislaus von Moos of the University of Zürich for his advice on the Hans Erni section; Mr Gilbert Hutin, director, and Mr Jean-Michel Matthey, sales director, at Hélio Courvoisier, for arranging and assisting my visit to the works at La Chaux-de-Fonds; the Dutch PTT, in particular Drs Marjan Vermeulen of the Communications Department, for permitting me to reproduce stamps issued by them after 1989 and for information on Dutch stamp designers; Mr Paul Hefting and Ada Lopes Cardozo in the Graphic Design section of the Dutch PTT in The Hague, the former for his encouragement and bibliographical suggestions, the latter for her useful comments on the Dutch section of the book; Prof Wim Crouwel and Anthon Beeke/Moir for permitting the reproduction of posters; Mr Denis Cromie at the GPO in Dublin, for permission to reproduce Irish stamps; Prof Leo Hoek, Amsterdam; Mrs Maureen Davey at Stanley Gibbons, London; Ian Whyte, Norman Clark, Gordon Davis, Desmond Norton in Dublin, for helping me to acquire many of the stamps illustrated; Brendan Dempsey, Trinity College Dublin, for his assistance with photography, and finally, Trinity College Dublin Association and Trust for a grant towards colour plates.

Front and back covers: Jean-Michel Foulon, Europa – Europa in Space, 1991 (Plate VIII, iii): Front and back inside covers: Edmund Dulac, unperforated sheets, 1943: Page 2; Hans Erni, Europa set, detail

First published in Great Britain in 1995 by
ACADEMY EDITIONS
an imprint of
ACADEMY GROUP LTD
42 Leinster Gardens, London W2 3AN
Member of VCH Publishing Group

ISBN: 1 85490 420 5

Copyright © David Scott 1995. *All rights reserved*
No part of this publication may be reproduced or transmitted in any form or by any means, whether by photocopying, recording or facsimile machine or otherwise howsoever without permission from the publishers.

Distributed to the trade in the USA by
NATIONAL BOOK NETWORK INC, 4720 Boston Way, Lanham, Maryland 20706

Printed and bound in Singapore

CONTENTS

DESIGNING SIGNS

THE STAMP AS A SIGN

Before exploring the conventions and scope of philatelic design, it is useful to examine the semiotic status of the postage stamp, to find out how the stamp is constructed and to explore its function as a sign. For signs to be read in the way intended by their designer, it is important to understand the semiotic characteristics of their component parts – text, image, image combination, format, colour, etc – and the way in which they interact to produce an overall effect. The stamp is an exceptionally complex sign in this respect both as a result of its scale and of its double function as a bearer of messages.

First of all, scale. The exceptionally small format of the stamp is in fact a mixed blessing from a design point of view. Perforation, which was introduced in British stamps in the 1850s, combined with a minuscule format, has the advantage of making any small vignette with such characteristics immediately recognisable as a stamp, although the drastically reduced surface area of the stamp image requires extreme concentration of component elements. Second, the stamp's dual function. The primary function of the stamp is to indicate the name of the country of the mail to which it is attached and the postage paid. This is the nature of the definitive stamp, which is the stamp normally used for regular mail and is usually of a small format and issued over a number of years. However, the stamp must also relay other types of message – the representative and 'commemorative' functions. The representative function is an extension of the definitive function in that it proposes a representative image of the country of issue in a way that is more visible and evocative than mere provision of the country's name. It usually takes the form of some identifying icon, a monarch's head, coat of arms, or a geographical or architectural feature. The stamp's commemorative function is usually signalled by a somewhat larger

Hans Erni, Switzerland, The World's Vacational Land, project for mural, Lucerne, 1939, 100x5m, detail. This mural illustrates many themes explored in Swiss commemorative stamps

format, one capable of accommodating commemorative as well as definitive messages. The 'Gentleman' format, evolved by David Gentleman in the late 1960s, is still the most common in British commemorative stamps today. Although more than twice the size of the definitive format, it nevertheless makes great demands of the designer who has to produce an image that is recognisable as a stamp, obeys the conventions agreed by the Universal Postal Union, and yet produces a distinctive image of the particular person, place or event commemorated on a given occasion.

The semiotic ambiguity of the postage stamp, particularly in relation to its multiple functions, is indicative of the more general difficulty of precisely defining the structure of signs.[1] Our understanding of visual signs has been increased enormously by the work at the turn of the century of the American philosopher Charles Sanders Peirce. The three classes of sign he defines in his *Second Trichotomy of Signs – Icons, Indices and Symbols*[2] are a valuable instrument of semiotic analysis, and consequently, I shall use them in the following way, first, to define the stamp's semiotic status and, second, to elucidate the rationale behind some philatelic design strategies.

Roughly translated, an icon is a pictorial sign; an index, a pointer sign; a symbol, a conventional sign. Whereas the stamp functions primarily as an *indexical* sign (pointing to the country of origin), as an object it encompasses *iconic* and *symbolic* elements (pictures, letters and numbers). Although the visual images the stamp adapts – such as portraits, monuments or landscapes – can be classed as icons, they may also function indexically like the maps, diagrams, logos or other schematic representations the stamp incorporates. In addition, the stamp uses symbols in

1a

1b

1c

the form of numbers, letters, names, acronyms or other linguistic or numerical elements incorporated into its design. However, as with other classes of sign, these are far from straightforward; context and interaction exert pressure on individual semiotic elements, causing them to take on functions that, in isolation, they would not adopt. A symbol, for example, can become an icon when it receives a noticeable degree of typographical definition or is placed in a prominent and isolated position.

The first function of the stamp is to identify a country, that is, to play an indexical role, thus forming a contiguous relationship with that country, to the extent that it is 'really affected by it', according to Peirce.[3] The stamp also functions as an index of the cost of postage of the letter or parcel and the fact that the price of postage has indeed been paid. The role of conventional symbols (primarily numbers and letters) in clarifying the indexical function is, of course, paramount. Indeed, the Universal Postal Union was set up in 1874 with the express purpose of agreeing, legislating and monitoring international conventions in relation to the postage stamp's indexical functions.

In addition to indicating a country, the second general function of the stamp is to represent that country, to 'afford information concerning its Object'[4]; in other words, to offer a symbolic representation of the country in traditionally recognisable terms. This is often achieved by incorporating an icon such as the profile of a reigning monarch, the national flag, an allegorical figure or national figurehead (for example, the French *Marianne*) or even an abbreviation of the country's name in some acronymic form. The pattern – format, iconic content, textual message – was established conclusively in 1840 with Sir Roland Hill's famous Penny Black stamp which showed the profile of Queen Victoria, the device 'Postage' and the face value of one penny (fig 1a shows the later, perforated 'Penny Red' version). The current British definitive stamp, displaying the portrait bust of Elizabeth II by Arnold Machin, continues this convention almost without change; issued over a quarter of a century ago in 1967, it is still current, having been converted to decimal currency in 1970-71 (fig 1b). The Penny Black's 150th anniversary was commemorated in Jeffery Matthews' simple but ingenious design of 1990 (fig 1c).

The third function of the stamp is to represent an aspect of a country. This is a more specific function, and one that operates within the more general representative function of the stamp in its definitive role. Here, the stamp appears to operate iconically; indeed, it may incorporate two sets of iconic signs. This is the function of the commemorative stamp, which although a secondary function, has become an increasingly important consideration in recent stamp design. In this case, the stamp, which is almost invariably pictorial, proposes a memento of an event, or anniversary of an object of national or international importance. If the event being commemorated is contemporary to the stamp's issue, the indexical role of the commemorative image is also significant. Today, by far the largest majority of stamps are commemorative and these are issued in a vast range of formats, colours and designs.

However, even when the stamp represents an aspect of a country, such as a monument or site, it equally represents the country itself, for the image reproduced on the stamp is accompanied by the signs which establish that nation's identity. Therefore, strictly speaking, the postage stamp is never, as Peirce would say, 'merely an Icon' or a picture; while representing an aspect of the reality of a country or a culture, it continues at the same time to represent the country as a national unit. This is its primary function. That is why the stamp – even when it incorporates iconic or pictorial elements on two or more semiotic levels, or even when these elements seem, as increasingly they do, almost to eclipse all other signs – remains, fundamentally, an indexical sign. It is interesting to explore this tension between iconic and indexical functions, particularly in relation to the development of stamp design strategies.[5]

1d

DESIGN STRATEGIES

The invention of company logos and the elaboration of corporate design strategies is a major area of activity for graphic design. The postage stamp, as an icon which both represents and promotes national identity, offers similar challenges to the designer, complicated by further requirements. These include the creation of an image susceptible to massive use and extensive exposure, and the elaboration of a symbolic form that is official, immediately recognisable, and also attractive and responsive to various modifications and permutations. A further demand is the necessity to express both the longevity and legitimacy of a particular culture or tradition and, at the same time, to assert its inherent flexibility and modernity in relation to a changing world.

1e

A major theme of this study is the quest by various European countries in the early part of this century, to establish a national icon which fulfils these multiple demands or, more recently, their search for the best means of presenting positively the history, tradition or other ideological notions attached to the nation's figurehead. This theme is illustrated in the way various designers adopt, modify or renew the solutions invented by their predecessors, and by the richness and the longevity of certain design conventions. Examples of these will be explored in particular in the first parts of Chapters One, Two and Four.

Anxious to capitalise on the iconic potential of what is essentially an indexical function in stamps, many countries have adopted a number of strategies calculated to iconise indexical elements in the design of the stamp. One strategy is to transform the essential symbolic element which clarifies the stamp's indexical function – the naming of the country of origin – into an icon of sorts. Thus, the acronym *RF* has often replaced the longer device *République française* on French stamps, turning it in fact into the logo of the country. For example, in Edmund Dulac's design *La Marianne de Londres* of 1945 (fig 1d), the acronym *RF* appears discreetly in the top left-hand corner of the stamp, balanced to the top right by the Cross of Lorraine, while the main part of the stamp is devoted to the profile of *Marianne*, the symbol of Liberty, the French Republic and the country France. The borders to either side of the *Marianne* figure are the olive branches symbolising the peace which followed the liberation of France in 1944. In this way, the strictly symbolic sign *RF* (reinstated after five years during which the stamps of the Vichy régime bore the caption *Postes françaises*), while maintaining its essential indexical function, also becomes a significant element in an iconic syntax conveying a specific ideological message, namely France's liberation and the re-establishment of Peace, Liberty and French Republican values after the humiliation suffered in World War II. A similar syntax of icons is identified in Edmund Dulac's George VI definitives of 1937, designed in collaboration with Eric Gill, where the monarch's head is framed with the floral symbols of the four constituent countries of the United Kingdom (fig 1e).

A second strategy used to iconise indexical elements in the stamp is that of pleonasm; the repetition of the indexical message in terms of icons. Thus, in the current French definitive stamp, the *Marianne du Bicentenaire*, created by Louis Briat to commemorate the Bicentenary of the French Revolution in 1989 (fig 2a), the symbolic elements indicating the stamp's country of origin (*République française*) and function (*La Poste*) are both aligned with and complemented by purely iconic motifs. The *Marianne* of 1989, with her Phrygian bonnet and Revolutionary

2a

2b

2c

2d

2e

3a   *3b*

3c   *3d*

cocarde, looks out at the viewer through three vertical bands of tone representing the French national flag, the tricolore. The message of the stamp is thus first read as a diagram of icons, only secondarily confirmed by the textual elements clarifying the stamp's indexical function; the verticality of the text's disposition, which makes it more difficult to read at a glance, seems to confirm this. The flag motif is, in fact, a common manifestation of semiotic pleonasm in stamps, as we can see in many Canadian and USA designs (figs 2b, 2c). The Canadian flag appeared in a spate of stamps in the late 1960s, issued around the time of the inauguration of its new form in 1965. This flag superseded the old one which incorporated the Union Jack. The US flag stamp marks the inclusion of the fiftieth state into the federation. The launch of a new flag or of a new state is often followed by issues of stamps incorporating the flag motif. This was the case with the many African states, formerly colonised by Britain, which achieved independence in the 1950s and 1960s. In a *Ghana* stamp of 1961 (fig 2d), the textual message confined by the stamp's designer to the margins of the frame, is rendered more or less superfluous by the iconic elements – the map of Africa showing Ghana, the profile of Elizabeth II, the national flag – which all convey the essential message of the stamp in visual terms. The text is embossed in dull gold with the effect that in some lights it disappears.

From the turn of the century through to the present day, Swiss definitive stamps offer a fascinating case history of the development of strategies promoting the iconisation of the indexical elements in philatelic design. Being a confederation of twenty-two cantons in which four different languages are spoken, the expression of national identity has always been a problem. As the stamps in fig 3 show, the national flag (a white cross on a red background, which is almost as well known in its reversed form as the symbol of the Red Cross) was used in a number of early designs, but usually backed up by further national icons – famous Swiss mountains such as the Jung Frau or the Mythen, or Helvetia. Helvetia offers the perfect illustration of the iconisation of an indexical or symbolic sign; on account of its four national languages (German, French, Italian, Romansch), Switzerland was obliged to adopt the Latin *Helvetia* to designate the Swiss federation on its stamps. This name, a symbol in Peircian terms, takes on the indexical function of indicating the stamp's country of origin, but its expressive power is also reinforced by personification as the figure or icon *Helvetia*. However, even this solution was not maintained beyond the 1920s, and was superseded by the national icon of a Swiss mountain landscape which had, except for Eugène Grasset's splendid high-value definitives of 1914, so far only appeared in the background of Swiss stamps, a foil to more conventional icons. From the 1930s to the 1960s, the landscape became the preferred image promoting Swiss national identity on stamps until it, in its turn, was relegated once again to the background of other themes such as architecture, post and telecommunications, and astrological signs. The ramifications of this topic will be explored more fully in Chapter Four.

The problem of establishing design coherence is also one that is raised in commemorative stamp design, for although each issue by definition involves a new set of images, establishing a distinct collective identity of the series of issues over a period of months or years is also a priority. This identity can be assured either singly or in combination, by format, printing style and by a number of internal graphic conventions. French commemorative issues from the 1920s onwards (for some examples, see Plate XI) were quick to establish such design coherence, producing, over the next half-century, beautiful one or two-colour, line-engraved issues in the double definitive format, collectable in the same way that prints and etchings used to be. The problem with this approach, however, was that after the

1950s, a certain common artistic patina was imposed on all issues, regardless of theme, so that atomic power and space exploration were expressed in the same style as historic or cultural events.

4b

The 1970s and the presidency of Valéry Giscard d'Estaing saw the legend *République française* being replaced by the more simple formula *France*, while attempts were made to vary printing techniques (photolithography was introduced as an alternative to recess engraving), colour range (multicolour was more widely used) and format (the introduction of other larger formats in addition to the successful 'masterpieces of art' series). However, overall developments were not well co-ordinated and for the first time a French stamp ceased immediately to be recognisable as such. A return to more traditional methods, including use of the device *République française,* has once again accompanied François Mitterrand's presidency, but, since 1981, as recent examples show (fig 4), French stamps have never regained the stylistic consistency they enjoyed before the 1970s. Stamps issued during the Bicentenary year of 1989, are an exceptional case and they will be discussed in detail in Chapter Two.

4c

4a

Through the adoption of the Gentleman format, and through high quality photographic reproduction techniques, British commemorative stamps in the same period succeeded in establishing a design profile that combined instant recognition with design flexibility. This was enhanced by the convention, established from the mid-1960s, of no longer identifying British stamps with the Dorothy Wilding portrait of the Queen but with a simple cameo profile of the royal head, printed in colour when not embossed in gold or silver. This simplified the task of fulfilling the stamp's indexical function, the head being placed, in theory, in the part of the stamp most suited to it on a given occasion. But what gives the British commemoratives from the 1970s onwards their particular design distinction is the way they subtly and variously draw to our attention the semiotic status of the images they propose, alerting us to the way graphic images are conceived, adapted and applied and the multiple visual sources from which they are drawn (fig 5). A more detailed exploration of this fascinating aspect of British commemorative stamp design will be made in Chapter One.

5a

This quality of semiotic sophistication is also much in evidence in Dutch stamp design since the early 1930s when the Dutch Post Office engaged some of the most talented graphic designers of the avant-garde movement to work on stamps. Chapter Three will explore the remarkable contribution designers such as Piet Zwart, Gerard Kiljan and Paul Schuitema made to philatelic design and the way their design strategies were adopted and applied systematically in Dutch stamps from the 1960s onwards.

5b

The difference between later developments in Dutch commemorative design and those in British is worth raising here since it obliges us to focus on a further fundamental issue relating not only to stamps but also to graphic design philosophy in general: that of legibility. From the 1920s onwards there have been two schools of thought, both within and without the avant-garde tradition, in relation to typography and graphic design. The first, perhaps the more traditionalist in outlook, has made clarity of message transmission the first priority in graphic or typographical design, placing it above all other considerations. Typefaces and illustrative elements (be they photographic, lithographic or engraved) should operate primarily as Peircian symbols; that is, as transparent signifiers through which the observer 'reads' the message. On the whole, this view has been held consistently by British stamp designers though, as their recent work has shown, it is far from being incompatible with extreme design sophistication and semiotic self-reflexivity.

5c

5d

5e

5f

6a

6b

6c

6d

6e

6f

6g

6h

The second school of thought, more consistently associated with avant-garde movements, stresses the importance of visual impact. In a world bombarded with messages, it is the form as much as the content which is at stake, and the typographical and illustrative elements should therefore work primarily as icons, that is as visual signs, only secondarily to be read and interpreted as messages. Although both attitudes are visible in Dutch stamp design, from the 1960s onwards, it is on the whole the iconic approach that has tended to dominate. The result of this is a commemorative stamp tradition in which in some instances the definitive functions of the stamp are almost occulted; sometimes the name of the country dances in diagonal leaps across the image (fig 6c), sometimes it is subsumed into the stamp's commemorative message, and it occasionally even appears upside down (fig 6h). In some recent designs, it is impossible to decide which way up the stamp should be viewed (figs 6b, 6d) while in others sophisticated and complex photomontage – sometimes using purely typographical elements – results in the presentation of the philatelic image more as a conundrum than a message (fig 6a). The Dutch predilection for smaller formats (until very recently, nothing as big as the Gentleman format) further promotes the illegibility of certain designs, many of which in fact look like posters reduced drastically in scale (figs 6e, 6f, 6g), which is not surprising in light of the fact that many Dutch stamp designers are also poster artists.

IDEOLOGICAL MESSAGES

The relative illegibility or ambiguity of commemorative stamp design can also, of course, be exploited for ideological purposes. An interesting example is the Irish stamp which in 1988 commemorated the 400th centenary of the Spanish Armada. Superficially, there is nothing obscure about this stamp (fig 7); it reproduces a handsome painting of the troop ship *Duquesa Santa Ana* specially commissioned by the Irish Post Office by the Irish artist Kenneth King, the son of Richard King, who designed many of the stamps of the Irish Free State in the 1930s and 1940s. The depiction of the ship is accurate historically and pictorially; it is fully laden with Spanish soldiers whose own ships had been shipwrecked on the coast of north-west Ireland; it is looking for the lee shore as it heads towards Scotland to pick up a further band of wrecked compatriots. However, it too came to grief soon after. The question to be asked here is not what are we looking at, but why, and at whose instigation?

1988 also saw a strip of five English stamps (fig 8) depicting the Spanish Armada, which commemorated a crucial year in English history; the year in which the might of Spain was crushed, the bluff of Philip of Spain called by Elizabeth I, and English naval superiority asserted. English pride in its naval glory and its love of pageantry are depicted lavishly in this set of stamps which, based on period images, shows the disastrous voyage of the Armada up the English Channel and into the North Sea. But what is the Irish stamp celebrating? The defeat of the Armada at the hands of the English, or its intentions – the wiping out of Protestantism in England? The stamp itself proposes no interpretation. It is a pure signifier, a 'mere icon', a vivid image. Instead of being proposed by the Irish philatelic committee, it was, rather exceptionally, commissioned by the Irish government. It is therefore a political stamp. But when we read the speech of the relevant Irish government minister at the opening of the 1988 Sligo symposium on the Spanish Armada, the political implications of this historic event are quite unclear, although capital is made of the opportunity with the usual commonplace claims of European unity promoted by the EC, which Ireland joined in 1973 along with Great Britain. The minister presiding at the stamp's launch was more specific:

It is fitting to remember and pay our respect to those seamen and soldiers who lost their lives, by the issue of a special commemorative stamp which will serve as a reminder of the past, and also of the fact that Ireland is today the custodian of the remains and reliquary of these wrecks around our coasts, which apart from being an invaluable source of information on the history of sixteenth-century ship construction, navigation and conditions of life at sea during that period, are a valuable part of our European cultural heritage and a link between Spain and Ireland.[6]

7

But what was the reception of the shipwrecked Spanish on Irish coasts in 1588? At the 1988 Sligo conference, the Spanish ambassador to Ireland read a paper which set out to question the general belief that Spanish survivors of Armada ships were cruelly treated by the native Irish — robbed, looted or slaughtered on the spot, if they were not handed over to English custody. He suggests that although the Irish often relieved the Spaniards of their worldly possessions, they did not harm them 'beyond what was strictly necessary for their purpose'.[7] For the Spanish and the Irish, the 1988 anniversary of the Armada was an opportunity to rewrite history in the context of developments in contemporary Europe. The Irish commemorative stamp commissioned for the occasion signals this while also serving as a discreet riposte to the unashamedly triumphalist message of the *British Armada* issue. But these ideological messages are not indicated specifically by the Irish stamp. The *décalage* between sign and signification leads to a reflection on the function of the stamp as a medium of cultural and ideological communication, one that I shall pursue in Chapters Two and Six in the context of France and post-colonial Ireland.

8

If ideological messages consistently prefer iconic to symbolic signs, images to words, it is because they often appeal first to irrational or unconscious impulses and are therefore less susceptible to criticism and objective analysis by the uninitiated viewer. They also permit a greater degree of ambiguity in their presentation of 'information concerning [their] Object'. The implications of this are worth pursuing, particularly in relation to the commemorative stamp whose role as a medium of cultural promotion continues to expand.

Despite its small size and relatively discreet support (letter or parcel), the stamp probably has a more concentrated ideological density per square centimetre than any other cultural form. Many countries have grasped this fact and some have created a stamp industry whose function is to produce a range of seductive images aimed at the collector. The issue of a triangular stamp, for example, is a certain sign that a country depends on philately for an important part of its revenue.

It is often the smallest countries that produce the largest number of stamps, which are often extravagant in their colour, format and imagery. Their aim is to create the illusion of a rich cultural identity. Hence, the stamps of Andorra, Monaco, Liechtenstein and San Marino give the impression that the cultural life of these little principalities is an endless succession of sports events, flower festivals or motor shows. Other small countries, such as the old British colonies, offer the collector a range of poetic visions of exotic flora and fauna, ceremonial rites and customs of primitive civilisations. The exquisite feeling for such subjects displayed by Michael and Sylvia Goaman in their designs for British colonial stamps (fig 9) will be explored in the second part of Chapter Five.

To the charms of theme and image must be added the seductions of form. The tiny format of the stamp works like a microcosm, offering a vision of the universe in which cultural and natural essences are concentrated. Sets of stamps offer the opportunity of creating a *musée imaginaire* of pictures, an anthology of poetic images. The stamp album becomes a kind of encyclopaedia, testifying to the

9

splendour and diversity of the world; it is knowledge encapsulated in an idealised, almost imaginary form. Similarly, stuck onto the envelope or parcel and franked by a distant mail office, the stamp offers the charm of a mysterious and exotic message, a fragment of another time and place sent to join us in our banal world. One of the first great stamp designers to explore the exotic potential of the colonial stamp, exploiting the brilliant colour made available by his use of modern photolithographic techniques, was Edmund Dulac. His work will be the subject of the first part of Chapter Five.

PEIRCIAN SEMIOTICS

While the primary emphasis in the ensuing chapters will be on design issues in stamps, the theoretical framework provided by Peircian semiotics will be used as a valuable instrument not only of definition and analysis but also of evaluation. This is because Peirce's distinction between iconic, indexical and symbolic signs provides a set of criteria against which both the authenticity and the functional efficiency of stamps as signs can be judged. For example, the undeniable appeal of the postage stamp as an 'exotic' image can be submitted to rigorous analysis in which the distinction between the stamp's iconic and indexical functions leads to an assessment of the authenticity of the icon(s) proposed by any given stamp. In this way it is possible to argue that Dulac's colonial or the Goamans' Commonwealth designs propose authentic icons of the countries on whose stamps they appear because they promote a real connection with the issuing state and are not merely glamorous images picked up from media, pop or other cultural sources. Offering authentic information about their countries of origin, these stamps are documents of enduring fascination and significance.

Similarly, the Peircian distinction between iconic and symbolic functions in signs becomes a useful tool in assessing the semiotic efficiency of stamps. This is a major concern in stamp design given the fact that the stamp is both an official sign and as such must be difficult to counterfeit, and a very small sign, albeit one that must be recognisable instantly. The role of typographical elements is important here. Letters are conventional signs – Peirce classes them as symbols – and are, in theory, relatively unambiguous in the messages they propose, at least within the restricted texts appearing on stamps. Their relationship with the icons promoted by the stamp, however, is potentially very complex. Semiotic efficiency is generally a function of the synchronisation of typographical and iconic components of the stamp design, whereby the two systems – iconic and symbolic – interact to reinforce the desired message. At the same time, the relative fluidity of Peirce's categories – he was quick to recognise, 'it would be difficult if not impossible, to instance an absolutely pure index, or to find any sign absolutely devoid of the indexical quality'[8] – serves to remind us that it is virtually impossible to define signs in absolute terms. This is especially true of signs as complex as postage stamps, in which the multiplicity of semiotic functions governing them and the variety of contexts in which they are used (or abused) leads one to adopt a wary approach. But the seemingly endless resourcefulness in exploiting sign components to various ends coupled with the ability to adapt to countless design strategies is part of the fascination of stamps. It is the aim of this book to explore the rich potential, both of stamps as signs, and of Peircian semiotic theory as a means of deepening our understanding of the structure and workings of sign systems.

Notes

1 Gérard Deledalle is the first semiologist to have tackled the problem of the postage stamp's semiotic status; see Chapter II of *Théorie et pratique du signe. Introduction à la sémiotique de Charles S Peirce*, Payot, Paris 1979, pp95-116.

2 Charles Sanders Peirce, *Collected Papers, Vol II Elements of Logic* (ed C Hartshorne and P Weiss), Belknap Press of University of Harvard, Cambridge, Mass, 1960, pp143-44.

3 *Collected Papers, Vol II*, p143.

4 *Collected Papers, Vol II*, p147.

5 The theoretical implications of these questions are explored further by David Scott in 'Semiotics and Ideology in Mixed Messages: the Postage Stamp' in *Word & Image Interactions II* (forthcoming 1995) and 'Stamp Semiotics: Reading Ideological Messages in Philatelic Signs' in *Proceedings of the 6th International Association of Semiotic Studies*, Mouton de Gruyter, 1995.

6 Draft of speech for the minister (Mr Ray Burke, TD) at the official stamp launch in 1988.

7 'Adventures and Misadventures of Captain Francisco de Cuellar in Ireland', a lecture delivered by His Excellency the Spanish Ambassador to Ireland, Dr José de Yturriaga, at the symposium on 'The Spanish Armada, Ireland and Europe', Sligo, September 1988, p14.

8 Charles Sanders Peirce, *Collected Papers*, p143.

Illustrations to Introduction

THE BRITISH TRADITION

(I) THE MONARCH'S HEAD: DEFINITIVE STAMPS 1840-1990

The adhesive, pre-paid postage stamp was invented in Britain by Sir Roland Hill in 1840. The first stamp, the Penny Black (fig1) appeared with the word *Postage* printed on it to signify its function, and the head of Queen Victoria adapted from Wyon's Guildhall Medal of 1838. Designed by Henry Corbould, it was engraved by Charles and Frederick Heath.[1] In Britain, the postal system is a royal organisation, the Royal Mail, which was founded in 1635. British stamps have always displayed the reigning monarch's head without any other indication of the country's name. Although the postage stamp is primarily an *indexical* sign – indicating country of origin, postage price and the fact that the postage has been paid – it often also incorporates an *icon*, in the case of British stamps, the monarch's head. This is done to facilitate rapid visual recognition of the country of origin and also to enhance the national profile.

Since 1840, the heads of six monarchs have appeared on English definitive stamps: Victoria, Edward VII, George V, Edward VIII, George VI and Elizabeth II (figs 2-8). During this one hundred and fifty year period, there have been about a dozen definitive designs: several under Victoria, of which three are commemorated in a set of stamps by David Gentleman issued in 1969 (fig 9); one for each of the four Kings, the two Edwards and the two Georges, plus one variation on George V (fig 4 designed by Bertram Mackennal and GW Eve) and two under Elizabeth II. During the long reign of Victoria, there was considerable experimentation with different types of image reproduction such as engraving, embossing and lithography (fig 9); however, from the 1930s, photogravure was for a long period adopted for lower value stamps, the great advantage of this technique being that a high standard of colour reproduction is assured. English stamps therefore have a brighter and denser colour than French stamps which, until recently, have mostly been recess printed.

The importance of the symbolism of the head is illustrated by the stamps commemorating the 100th and 150th anniversaries of the postage stamp's invention. The centenary fell during the reign of George VI and was marked by an issue carrying the head of George VI and the head of Victoria that had appeared on the first postage stamp in 1840 (fig 10). The same method, which was no doubt inspired by an essay of Edmund Dulac, dating from 1940, was used in 1990 by Jeffery Matthews for the 150th anniversary in which the head of Elizabeth II was juxtaposed with that of Victoria (fig 11).

The symbolism of British definitive stamps has always been discreet; for the most part, the monarch's head has sufficed. From 1901, however, with the coronation of Edward VII, the royal head was surmounted by, or associated with the imperial crown (figs 2-6). The crown disappears from British stamps with the ascension of Elizabeth II, although it is retained in the form of the St Edward's crown in many British colonial stamps. Elizabeth II's image was represented on stamps by the Dorothy Wilding photographic study which portrays the Queen wearing a tiara (fig 12). The crown is replaced by motifs symbolising the four countries which constitute the United Kingdom: the English rose, the Welsh daffodil, the Scottish

1840 first engraved issue

1847 first embossed issue

1855 first surface printed issue

Opposite: The royal bust, based on a cast by Arnold Machin for the second Elizabethan definitive series

12

14

15

16

thistle and the shamrock of Northern Ireland. These motifs are integrated into the design of the stamp as a garland or sprigs encircling the royal head (figs 7 and 15). In the second Elizabethan definitive series, however, the royal bust, based on a cast by Arnold Machin (fig 13), appears alone, along with the surface value of the stamp (fig 8, decimal version, fig 16). In the regional versions of this stamp, however, the heraldic symbol of each country is reinstated; the Welsh dragon, the Scottish lion *marchant* and the Red hand of Ulster for Northern Ireland, in each case juxtaposed with the royal head (fig 17a-c). Although never used on UK stamps, Pietro Annigoni's portrait of the Queen of 1954-55 (fig 14), has been much used on British colonial issues.

Although, in comparison with the French *Marianne*, the representation of the monarch seems scarcely to vary, the monarchy has often been used thematically in British commemorative stamps marking coronations, royal marriages, anniversaries and, more recently, the marriages of royal princes and princesses. The 60th birthday of the Queen in 1986, for example, was marked by two stamps in which six photos of the Queen marked successive decades of her life (fig 19) while the silver wedding anniversary of the Queen's marriage to Prince Philip was commemorated in 1973 with a design based on a photo by Norman Parkinson (fig 18). The 25th anniversary of her coronation was marked in 1978 by a series of stamps which show in gold the attributes of royal power (fig 20), another set designed by Jeffery Matthews, who has been entrusted with many royal themes in British stamps. This set shows the form of the royal effigy used by commemorative stamps since 1966.

The great advantage of using the monarch's head as a national symbol is that it can be used both as an icon and as an index, as both a definitive and a commemorative image. In the 1986 set (fig 19) it is the right-hand side photograph in both instances that marks the stamps as British, while at the same time integrating itself into the commemorative message of the stamp (six successive images of the Queen, each marking a decade of her life). Similarly, in the 1992 set marking the fortieth anniversary of the Queen's accession in 1952 (plate I, v), her photograph both identifies the country issuing the stamp and is a major thematic motif in the stamp's message (five successive images of her reign). In addition, the option of positioning the monarch's head in the foreground, as either a definitive image in standard definitive stamps or as a commemorative image within anniversary stamps, or both (as just shown in figs 18-19 and plate I), is further supplemented by the option of using the small version of the Queen's profile, based on Mary

13

Gillick's coinage head, as the identifying icon in British commemorative stamps. This method, which has been adopted as the norm since the mid 1960s, allows the design maximum freedom and flexibility in exploiting the stamp format.[2]

The development of photogravure processes of reproduction in the twentieth century made available new possibilities to stamp designers, especially in the area of image clarity and colour density. Before the 1930s, stamps had mostly been engraved, using a variety of recess or typographic processes, resulting in the 'lined' effect so clearly evident in earlier stamps. Great Britain was one of the first countries to exploit the possibilities of photogravure in stamp design, starting in 1934 with a revised set of George V definitives. This was followed in 1936 by photo-based definitive stamps showing the new King Edward VIII (fig 5, photo by Hugh Cecil), although the design simplicity of this issue gave rise to considerable controversy. In 1937, the definitive stamps of George VI's reign (fig 6) continued the simplicity of the 1936 formula, but with greater refinement of detail, especially in the lettering by Eric Gill, and the drawing of the head by Edmund Dulac. From the 1960s onwards, photographs were increasingly used to commemorate royal or recent historical figures, with matching simplicity of presentation. From the 1980s, British commemorative stamps have exploited effectively the potential both of regular portrait photography – as in John Gorham's design commemorating the Queen Mother's ninetieth birthday in 1990 (fig 21), and sophisticated photomontage techniques, as in Why Not Associates' 1992 design (plate I, v). Commemorative stamps are issued for a short period of time to mark specific events or to commemorate important anniversaries. Their larger format permits greater design flexibility and sophistication than that available to definitive stamps, which are usually smaller. A feature of British commemorative stamps issued since the adoption of decimal currency in 1971 and the standardisation of the larger format designed by David Gentleman, has been the invitation to the stamp's viewer to enter into and appreciate the design process itself as well as the theme or object being commemorated. Such involvement has been made possible by the use of the cameo Queen's head, thus permitting minimal interference in the design of the stamp's definitive or indexical function, and the standardisation of formats (the Gentleman model was supplemented in the 1980s by a squarer alternative). The rest of this chapter explores the strategies developed by British stamp designers in creating original and self-reflexive commemorative images.

17

18

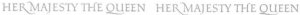

19

20

21

(II) MEDIUM AS MESSAGE
RECENT COMMEMORATIVE STAMPS 1971-1994

DESIGN STRATEGIES
Image within Image

In stamps of this kind (plate II), the designers invite us to participate in the design process by reminding us that we are seeing the *representation of a representation*, an image of an image, or by pointing out through visual clues the image status of what we are looking at. In other words, as well as presenting an attractive icon, the stamp also indicates the manner in which icons are constructed and alerts us to the processes involved in viewing images. For example, in L Trickett's 1988 *Christmas* set (plate II, ii), the card on the stamp indicates the likely contents of the envelope – a Christmas card. Here, the stamp works as an indexical sign (a pointer) as well as an iconic sign (an image). In Michael Dempsey's 1988 *Europa – Transport and Mail* set (plate II, iii), the unfurled corners of the poster remind the viewer that he or she is looking at the image of an image, while in Maddox, Trickett and Webb's *Urban Renewal* design of 1984 (plate II, i), the plan or map unfurls across the image of that to which it corresponds in reality. Meanwhile, the tears, overlaps and repetitions in the image in Daniel Fern's 1989 *Europa – Games and Toys* set, similarly draw our attention to the image status of the stamp (plate II, iv). The use of monochrome in Delaney Associates' *The Age of Steam* set of 1992 (plate II, v), confirms the photographic base on which all images in this set are constructed.

Specimens and Fragments

In stamps of this kind, the viewer is offered an almost unaltered glimpse of the object being represented. All the designer has to do – although this is the skilful part – is select and frame the given image or fragment. For example, in the Peter Hatch Partnership set commemorating British Textiles, the viewer browses through the samples offered like a customer in a draper's store (plate III, ii), while in Howard Brown's prize-winning set marking the Bicentenary of the Ordnance Survey (plate III, iii), fragments of four maps from four different dates are used to plot the changes in an English village. With such designs, there is no need for textual accompaniment or explanation; the image speaks for itself.

Paintings and Prints, Book Illustrations

Another formula used in Britain since 1967 is to take a painting, print or illustration and to convert it for use as a philatelic image simply by adding the Queen's head, coloured or embossed in gold, and the face value of the stamp. The great advantage of this is the inherent simplicity and minimal interference with the image depicted. This is particularly important where the image itself is based on a work of art. Stuart Rose designed several sets of this kind (for example, plate IV, i). Book illustrations can be adapted to stamps in a similar way and the illusion of period book illustration can be created.

In his 1979 set marking the International Year of the Child (plate IV, iii), E Hughes recreates effectively the child's world by making a collage of illustrations from four famous English childrens' authors, while M Swartridge and S Dew, in their *Centenary of the Death of Edward Lear* series (plate IV, iv), reproduce images from Lear's *Nonsense Songs* and other sources on creamy white, album-like pages. In an unusually large, elongated format, Andrew Davidson's *Sherlock Holmes*

1993 set (plate IV, v), reproduces not only scenes from Conan Doyle's famous detective stories but also simulates the steel engraved images used to illustrate early editions of the books.

Visual Metonymies

A metonymy is a rhetorical figure in which a part is taken for the whole. Its aim is to increase the suggestiveness or impact of the part thus isolated, enabling it, paradoxically, to express more than the whole for which it stands. Visual adaptations of this principle can work very effectively, particularly within confined dimensions. This section explores the scope of visual metonymy in postage stamp design. In John Gibbs's *International Year of the Disabled* set (plate V, ii), the focus on the functioning limbs of the disabled persons depicted elicits sympathy and understanding while also producing remarkably poetic images (18p, 25p); while in N Cudworth's 1986 *Sports* set (plate V, iv), the focus is where it should be – on the calves, knees, stomach muscles, wrists and biceps that take the strain in the activities depicted. David Gentleman's talent as a designer is particularly evident in his creation of visual metonymies, as can be seen in his *Social Reformers* set of 1976 (plate V, i) and the 1982 series commemorating the death of Darwin (plate V, iii).

Palimpsest and Collage

Techniques by which images can be superimposed, wholly or in fragments, singly or multiplied, are used in particular by stamps attempting to express the complex or multiple achievements of an age, period or organisation. In Newell and Sorrell's 1984 set, the human face of the British Council is superimposed on the texts (chemical formula, musical score, architectural plan, dictionary definition) that constitute British science and culture (plate VI, i), while in Michael Dempsey's and C Slaine's 1987 design commemorating the *150th Anniversary of Queen Victoria's Accession* (plate V, iii), a collage of images of the Victorian age is juxtaposed with portraits of the ageing monarch, the style of image presentation and framing reflecting Victorian scrapbook design.

EXPRESSING CONCEPTS

If handled with imagination, the tiny format of the postage stamp is able to express quite complex scientific, technological, cultural or other concepts. British stamp designers have managed this by exploiting the small but subtle variations in format available (square, elongated, vertical and horizontal rectangular) and, especially, by exploiting some of the design strategies illustrated in the previous section. Sarah Godwin's *Newton* set of 1987, for example (plate VII, iv) explores various Newtonian theories relating to mathematics, gravity, motion and optics, by juxtaposing textual and geometrical formulae with visual images ranging from the proverbial apple to a modern space telescope. Economies of scale are explored effectively in H Waller's 1984 set commemorating the *Centenary of the Greenwich Meridian* (plate VII, i), in which the scale moves stamp by stamp from planetary to life-size dimensions.

The British Post Office's choice of designers from different graphic or artistic spheres was an astute move in relation to providing insights into certain concepts. In 1986, Ralph Steadman, the famous illustrator and caricaturist, was invited to share his vision of how comets operate within the planetary system (plate VIII, iv), while the Belgian artist, Jean-Michel Folon explores the psychological and the scientific or technological aspect of the space concept in his designs for the *Europa, Europe in Space* issue (plate VIII, iii). Instead of depicting the predictable bits of hardware floating in space offered by most Europa stamp issues exploring

The Black Prince 1330/1376

22

Owain Glyndŵr c1354/1416

Robert the Bruce 1274/1329

Henry the Fifth 1387/1422

this theme, Folon presents an altogether more imaginative perspective. For another *Europa* series, *Protection of the Environment*, 1993 (plate VIII, v), it was appropriate that the Post Office invite young children, those who will most likely suffer from the environmental disasters bequeathed to them by the twentieth century, to express their reactions to ecological problems. As with work of most children, the designs are bright and disturbing. The problem of how to express visually, in a few square centimetres, a concept as elusive as music was also imaginatively resolved by Wilson McLean in his 1985 *Europa* set commemorating European Music Year (plate VIII, i). Where many European countries contented themselves with producing stamps showing banal portraits of famous musicians, McClean attempts the more difficult but rewarding task of expressing in visual terms the kinds of images that flit through the mind when music is heard. The use of an inverted image to express the reflection in water of angelic musicians was a bold and effective ploy in the context of Handel, as was the wing over the water for Elgar's *Sea Pictures* (plate IX, iii).

IMAGES OF HISTORY

History, cultural history and natural history are among the themes stamps have always expressed best, offering as they do a window to the world through which a country's artistic, scientific and other qualities can be displayed persuasively. The British love of pageantry is much in evidence in recent issues commemorating historical events, for example, Fritz Wegner's medieval warriors commemorated in 1974 (fig 22), sea battles such as the defeat of the Armada, (see introductory chapter, fig 8) and the industrial revolution as evoked by David Gentleman in his *150th Anniversary of the Liverpool and Manchester Railway* set of 1980 (fig 23).

The stamps commemorating aspects of natural history such as Pandora Sellers' *Orchid* set of 1993 (plate X, iii) or David Gentleman's *Swan* series (plate X, iv) show how sensitive water-colour drawings against a white background are more effective than photographs in the depiction of flora and fauna. The variety of graphic styles employed by the stamp designers showing facets of British cultural history reflects the various traditions that have flourished within the latter. In her set commemorating the 400th anniversary of the birth of Inigo Jones of 1973 (plate IX, i), Rosalind Dease uses original drawings to illustrate the multi-faceted talent of one of Britain's greatest architects and designers, while Fritz Wegner organises traditional and picturesque shapes into coherent designs in his 1981 *Folk Customs* set (plate IX, ii). Contrasting ways of portraying vegetation are illustrated in Liz Butler's and P Leith's designs celebrating British gardens and Kew respectively (plate IX, iii and iv).

23

Notes

1   The history of stamp design has been fully explored; for succinct accounts see William Finlay, *An Illustrated History of Stamp Design*, Peter Lowe, London 1974, pp13-18, and Stuart Rose, *Royal Mail Stamps: a survey of British stamp design*, Phaidon, London 1980, pp31-48.

2   The relative reduction in size and then simplification of the royal portrait (the substitution of Wilding photograph by the cameo profile, based on the Mary Gillick coinage head) constituted an important development in the history of British commemorative stamp design. It is documented in Stuart Rose, *Royal Mail Stamps: a survey of British Stamp design*, pp57-66.

10

11

NATIONAL ICONS
The French Stamp

(1) VARIATIONS ON MARIANNE *1850-1992*

The dual nature of the postage stamp, analysed above using semiotic terms, can be further defined in terms of rhetorical categories. As we have seen, the stamp as an icon manifests metonymic tendencies, that is, it offers an image which represents a part rather than the whole of an object or a reality. As a symbol, it tends towards the metaphorical. Because of its reduced format and the heavy load of symbols or emblems it carries (the representation of a country or a specific aspect of a country, or both), it tends to propose fragments of images, emblems, logos or other abbreviations, or syntheses of various kinds of allegorical figures. These forms are amalgamations of elements which, when brought together and abbreviated, represent a complex reality such as a company, an institution, a country.

As on bank notes (many of which are designed by stamp artists and engraved by the same companies that print stamps), the head becomes a principal motif of the postage stamp. As we saw, in Britain, no name appears on the country's stamps; the monarch's head is sufficient to identify the country, which being the first to use stamps of this kind, needs nothing else to establish national identity. Although France is obliged to indicate in writing the stamp's country of origin, there have however been attempts to transform this written message into a more compact formula, either by using abbreviations such as *Repub Franc* as on the first French stamp of 1849 (fig 1a), or the acronym *RF* (see fig 1e), which (in the twentieth century) has virtually become the country's logo. The different ways the country has been named – *République française* and *Empire français*, under Napoleon III (fig 2); *Postes françaises* under the German Occupation 1940-44 (fig 4); and *France* beneath Giscard d'Estaing, 1974-81 (fig 15a) – reflect the different political ideologies of the country's successive governments. In the following study, I shall examine both recurrent iconic elements in French definitive stamps over the last one hundred and forty years and the development of the commemorative stamp in France since its introduction in the first decades of this century. In doing so I shall try to clarify the image that France offers to the world through its stamps, to pinpoint the philatelic icons of French nationhood and show the extent to which they have changed over the last century and a half.

France has presented itself to the world in its definitive stamps using more than thirty different national icons over the last one hundred and forty years. The list includes about a dozen *Mariannes* (from 1944 to today) two *Coq gaulois* (1944 and 1962-65); Jean-Jacques Barre's *Ceres* (with several variations dating from 1849 to 1941); Oscar Roty's *Semeuse* or sower (with several variations from 1903 to 1960-61); Muller's *Moissonneuse* or harvester of 1954 (fig 13), and several more conventional allegorical figures including Jules-Auguste Sage's *Paix et Commerce* or Peace and Commerce of 1876-1900 (fig 3b); Luc-Olivier Merson's *Marianne* of 1900-24 (fig 3a); Joseph Blanc's *Amour et Justice* or Love and Justice of 1900-24 (fig 3c); Eugène Mouchon's *Droits de l'homme* or Rights of Man of 1900-24 (figs 3d-e); PA Laurens' *Paix* or Peace of 1932-33 (fig 8a); G Hourriez's *Mercure* or Mercury, 1938-41,

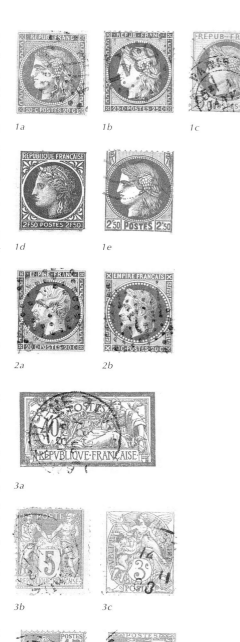

1a   1b   1c

1d   1e

2a   2b

3a

3b   3c

3d   3e

Opposite: Nanine Vallain, La Liberté, 1793, courtesy Musée de la Révolution Française Vizille; Eugène Delacroix, La Liberté aux barricades, 1830 (courtesy of the Réunion des Musées Nationaux)

4a

4b

4c

4d

4e

5a

5b

5c

5d

5e

6a

6b

7

8a

8b

8c

(fig 8b) and Iris, 1939 (fig 8c); Gandon's *Liberté* after Delacroix, 1982-89 (fig 12); and *Sabine* after Louis David, the stamp of Giscard d'Estaing's *France*, 1977-81 (fig 15a).

In addition to such imaginary or mythological figures, French definitive stamps have also shown three real or historical persons on their stamps. These are: Louis-Napoléon (Napoléon III from 1852-70, figs 2a and 2b) as created by Albert Barre, son of Jean-Jacques, the designer of the first *Ceres*; Louis Pasteur from 1923-26, engraved by Prud'homme (fig 7); Maréchal Pétain (1941/42-44), as designed by Jules Piel in 1941 (fig 4a), by Frost, Lemagny and Bersier from 1941-42 (figs 4b-d) and by Bouguenec in 1942 (fig 4e). Apart from the period of the Second Empire between 1850-70, when the profile of Napoléon III appeared on French stamps (see figs 2a and 2b), and the years of German occupation during the Second World War from 1940-44, when various different designs incorporating the profile of Pétain were issued (figs 4a-e), France has been a republic. Having had no monarch since 1848, the French, unlike their German and Italian neighbours who are also republican, have sought alternative symbols or figures to represent their identity and national aspirations. The country has tended notably towards the selection of female figures, often associated with maternity or the earth, and almost always, in one way or another, associated with the figure of *Marianne*, symbol of Liberty, the Republic and the French nation.

The first national icon of this kind to be reproduced on a French stamp, and in fact, the first French stamp, was JJ Barre's *Ceres* (fig 1), Roman goddess of agriculture. The *Ceres* figure was chosen in part, no doubt, for its regular Roman profile which adapts well to insertion in a small format (*Ceres's* head appeared on many Roman coins). It was also chosen for the discreet but evident symbolism incorporated into the design – a swathe of wheat and a bunch of grapes or a garland of laurels. *Ceres* appeared several times on French stamps between 1849 and 1941[1], the 1938 and 1945 versions (figs 1d and 1e) being designed by G Hourriez and C Mazelin. The *Semeuse* (fig 5) and *Moissonneuse* (figs 13a-b) by Muller, issued in 1954 and 1960, are two other types which illustrate the agricultural wealth of France.

The first, designed by Oscar Roty, has become a classic image, having been retained over twenty years at the beginning of the century, and having also appeared on French coins. In the stamp versions, the graceful but solid profile of the woman (whose Phrygian bonnet relates her to *Marianne)* has been enhanced by its presentation either as a cameo, against a background of engraved lines or with her feet on earth. In one version of the stamp, the sun is seen to be rising in the distance while in the 1960-61 version, the *Semeuse* is redesigned by J Piel. Another figure associated with agriculture and country life reproduced on French stamps is that of the *Coq gaulois* (see figs 6a and 6b). This image was used to announce, like the coming of dawn, the liberation of France in 1944. It was taken up again by Albert Decaris in his stamp of 1960; this stamp was the first French definitive stamp to use more than two colours. Like one of the *Semeuse* designs, Decaris' *Coq* appears against the background of the rising sun (fig 6b). The link between *Marianne* and the *Coq gaulois* is confirmed both in the essay by J-C Mathias for a definitive stamp to mark the Bicentenary of the French Revolution in 1989, which superimposes the cock motif on the profile of *Marianne* (plate XV, v), and Gérard Garouste's stamp of 1992 commemorating the Bicentenary of the French republic, in which *Marianne*, the *Coq gaulois* and a sheaf of wheat are combined in one startling image (fig 16b). Other mythical types used by French stamps between 1849 and 1941 include the aforementioned *Paix et Commerce*, *Amour et Justice*, *Droits de l'homme*, *Paix*, *Mercure* and *Iris*.

Although they do not decorate airmail stamps, *Iris* and *Mercure*, the winged messengers of the Gods, make their appearance on French stamps at the time in the late 1930s when aircraft were playing an increasingly important role in the delivery of mail.[2] Mouchon's design incorporating the *Droits de l'homme* theme (the two versions of it are illustrated in figs 3d and 3e) is particularly interesting from a semiotic point of view. The stamp depicts the woman, who is an allegorical representation of France, holding in her hands a tablet on which are engraved the rights of man. The visual image and the visual emblem are both framed and underlined by the device *République française* which appears at the bottom of the stamp and which therefore indicates both the provenance of the stamp and the ideology of the nation which issued it. This indexical use of the country as naming device to support the iconic sign of the allegorical figure holding the sacred tablet with its message of political freedom, is one that is exploited in a number of stamps marking the Bicentenary of the French Revolution in 1989.

The image which has since the Second World War established itself in the world of French stamps as the foremost national icon is of course that of *Marianne* (fig 9).[3] Nickname of the French Republic and symbol of Liberty, *Marianne* takes the form of a woman of ample bosom whose Phrygian bonnet attests to her democratic origins – Roman slaves released from captivity wore a Phrygian cap as a mark of their freedom. Her form and most of her symbolic attributes (which are classed in themes or documented in some French stamps of 1989-90 marking the Bicentenary of the French Revolution) derive from various allegorical types, in particular *Liberty* as depicted in the paintings, sculptures and engravings of the 1780s and 1790s, such as Nanine Vallain's *La Liberté* of 1793 (fig 10) and later, Delacroix's *La Liberté aux barricades* of 1830 (fig 11) on which Gandon's 1981 stamp is based (fig 12). Having made her debut discreetly in Merson's design of 1900 and in the *Semeuse* of 1903, *Liberty* reappears in the foreground in 1944. In the *Algiers* series (fig 9a), issued at the time of the liberation of France, she is crowned with laurels, while in Edmund Dulac's design of 1945, the *London* series (fig 9b), she is framed in the garlands of victory.[4] She appears in her most classic form in the late forties in the head created by one of France's most famous stamp designers, Pierre Gandon, typographed in the lower values (fig 9c), recess printed in the higher (figs 9d-e); this is the form in which she appears for most of the next ten years. Wearing a Phrygian bonnet but without any further ornamentation, she is framed in a stamp, the three textual elements of which are kept to a strict minimum; they comprise the acronym of the country – *RF*; the device *Postes* and the face value, plus, in minuscule letters in the margin, the name of the artist and the engraver. She is replaced in 1955 by the *Marianne* designed by Muller (fig 9f); here, her profile is picked out against a background of the rising sun, and she is crowned with oak leaves. In 1959, she appears on a boat as *Marianne à la nef* by Regaganon (fig 9g) and in 1960, in a design by Decaris, her profile in grey on a dark red background is decorated with laurels and a sheaf of wheat (fig 9h). The witty *Marianne* invented by Jean Cocteau followed in 1961 (fig 9i); here she sports the Phrygian bonnet with a tricolour rosette on a background of wheat sheaves and the French coat of arms. She is followed in turn in 1967-69 by Cheffer's *Marianne* whose beautiful sculpted head is again decorated with wheat sheaves (fig 9j). In 1971 a Phrygian bonnet reappears on the head of the *Marianne* designed by Raoul Béquet (see fig 9k).

A new symbolic orientation is offered by the French stamp after 1977 when the right-wing government of Valéry Giscard d'Estaing launched the *Sabine* image (fig 15a). This fine head derives from David's famous painting *The Sabine Women*, but appears of a more smiling disposition on the stamp than on David's canvas.

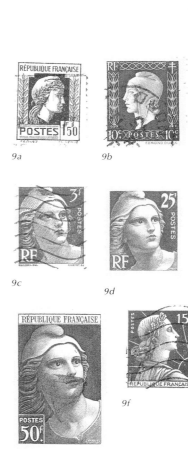

9a *9b*

9c *9d*

9f

9e

9g *9h*

9i

9j *9k*

12a *12b*

13a *13b*

14

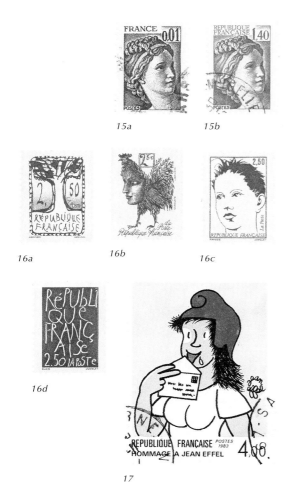

15a   15b

16a   16b   16c

16d

17

The device *France* replaces that of *République française* for the first time on a French definitive stamp although it had already been used on numerous commemorative stamps from the 1920s (plate XI, ix). However, the *France* etiquette was relinquished in favour of *République française* (fig 15b) after the defeat of Giscard d'Estaing's party in 1981 and the election of the Socialist government under François Mitterrand. Another riposte of the latter, designed further to announce the reinstatement of the republican tradition, was the restoration of the *Marianne* image, based on Delacroix's painting *La Liberté aux barricades* (fig 11). This stamp appeared in 1982 (fig 12) and presided over the decade until 1989, the Bicentenary of the French Revolution, when, after a national competition, it was replaced by the *Marianne* designed by Louis Briat (fig 14). Among the designs short listed for the stamp (plate XV), the visual motifs traditionally associated with France – the Phrygian bonnet, Revolutionary rosette, the *Coq gaulois* – are still much in evidence. Briat's design succeeds in incorporating not only *Marianne* in a Phrygian bonnet decorated with the revolutionary rosette but also, and this despite the monochrome of the design, a suggestion of the French national flag, the *Tricolore*, through the three vertical bands of which the face of *Marianne* looks out towards the viewer. Briat has also minimised the impact of the symbolic and indexical elements of the design in favour of the iconic by aligning the latter vertically with the bands of shading. Thus the viewer reads *Marianne's* face and conventional emblematic attributes before seeking textual confirmation that this is indeed a postage stamp (*La Poste*) of French origin (*République française*). Once again, iconic elements are brought to the foreground at the expense of indexical signs, even in what is a definitive, as opposed to a commemorative stamp.

France's concern, one might even say obsession, with the imaginary figure of *Marianne* is also illustrated by a set of four stamps issued in 1992 to commemorate the Bicentenary of the French republic. To mark this event, three famous contemporary French and one Belgian artist – Pierre Alechinsky – were commissioned to produce images expressing this theme. In the event, two of designs turned out to be variations on *Marianne*.

The stamp mentioned above, by Gérard Garouste (born in 1946), incorporates *Marianne* into a synthesis of national icons (fig 16b), while Martial Raysse (born in 1936), reinvents *Marianne* as a contemporary French woman, of boyish looks, with her hair cropped short (fig 16c). The tendency towards a parody of *Marianne* – who was herself born in the nineteenth century as a figure of fun, used by

18a   18b

200ᵉ Anniversaire de la Proclamation de la République

1792 - 1992

16a,b

16c,d

19

20

21

22

23

conservatives and reactionaries to ridicule Republican tendencies – is also illustrated in the stamp celebrating the caricaturist Jean Effel, whose speciality, as the stamp shows, was in sending up *Marianne* (fig 17).

Marianne has also appeared consistently on French commemorative stamps, especially in the 1930s when she was used as an allegorical symbol of France in a number of issues involving promotion of charities or national and international agreements. In 1935, in a stamp by Grégoire, she promotes the Unemployed Intellectuals Relief Fund (fig 19), while in Ouvré's design of 1936 she exhorts support for the Public Health Fund (fig 20). Later in the same year, in a design by Barlingue, she shakes hands with the United States (fig 21) in a stamp commemorating the 150th anniversary of the American constitution, while in 1938 her hand shakes that of *Britannia* in a design by Cheffer marking the politically highly significant visit to Paris by George VI and his Queen (fig 22). It is appropriate that similar symbolism should have been used in the two *se tenant* pairs of stamps issued in 1994 to commemorate the opening of the Channel Tunnel. Of the two designs, the first by the British artist George Hardie shows the British Imperial lion clasping the claw of the *Coq gaulois,* while the French design by Jean-Paul Cousin shows *Marianne* and *Britannia* sporting appropriate rosettes on their fingers, linking hands over the English Channel (figs 18a-b).[5]

More generally, *Marianne* has been used to symbolise the national patrimony, as in Forget's design of 1980 (fig 23) in which *Marianne's* image, based on Gandon's design of 1945, is slotted into the commemorative format in a similar way to that of the Queen's head on British designs of the 1950s and early 1960s. A proto-image of *Marianne*, an allegorical representation of the new French republic, is used in Marie-Noëlle Goffin's design (fig 24), based on an *assignat* of the French revolutionary period, to commemorate the republic's Bicentenary in 1992, while Gandon's adaptation of Delacroix's *Liberté* of 1830 to the definitive stamp of Socialist France of the 1980s, is itself adapted in two successive stamps, issued in 1987 and 1988, announcing the Philexfrance exhibition organised to coincide with the Bicentenary celebrations in Paris in 1989 (figs 25 and 26).

France has consistently used commemorative stamps to promote its cultural and scientific achievements in a distinctive way. First, a definitive stamp, slightly modified or even simply overprinted with a supplementary sign was used, as in the red cross surcharge issue of 1914 based on the *Semeuse* (fig 5d). Then, new

24

25

26

designs appeared within the small definitive framework. The first in France were Surand and Dumoulin's designs for the War Orphans' Fund in 1917 (fig 27 shows the lowest value by Dumoulin). Design quickly improved, no doubt in part inspired by more cheerful subject matter, as in Rigal's 1930 design for the International Colonial exhibition (fig 28). However, before long the advantages of a larger framework became apparent and, in France, a double definitive framework was adopted from 1917-18 for an increasing number of stamps (plate XI). The advantage of the double format was the opportunity it offered to present images horizontally in the 'landscape' format or vertically as 'portraits'. Most French commemorative stamps have since become, in effect, either landscapes (including towns, sites and monuments) or portraits (French men and women of historical or cultural importance).

27

In the last twenty years, a greater variety of formats has been introduced (plate XII). Once again, these enlarged formats reflect conventional means of artistic representation. Thus, the very large format – landscape or portrait – is used for the series of stamps promoting great works of French art (plate XII, Yves Klein) and the extra-wide landscape format, which is the equivalent of three standard definitive stamps, is used to present extensive landscape views (plate XII, *La Brenne*). The importance of maintaining the artistic tradition in French culture is also indicated by the use of stamps which, until the 1970s at any rate, were line-engraved rather than photographically reproduced. This custom of using typography and, later, engraving as a means of reproduction attached French stamps to a long-established tradition in Europe. For France, the commemorative stamp was almost immediately conceived as a miniature engraving to be collected as prints or etchings were collected. It was this, plus the relative consistency of themes extolled, that gave the French stamp its distinctive style from the 1930s through to the 1960s. Since the early 1990s, however, there has been a marked change in commemorative design in France. The adoption of photographic methods and the much greater design freedom allowed, has resulted in wittier and more playful images that have far more in common with British and Dutch design. The Good Luck stamp (fig 30) reflects contemporary British greetings stamps while the diagonal typography and asymmetric design of the Marcel Cerdan stamp (fig 29) based on a photograph of 1948 and the typographic style of the Louvre commemoratives 1993 (fig 32) both reflect the influence of recent Dutch stamp design.

28

29

30

31

32

DE FRANSCHE VRYHEID.

Zie hier het Echt toneel der Fransche Vryheyds Zoonen,
   Moord - plundering - geweld, en Schenden van den Stoet
Der Maagden, zal ons hier, haar snooden inborst toonen,
   Og Arme haan, zwijg stil, - straks valt uw Vryheids Hoed.

33

32

(II) COMMEMORATING THE BICENTENARY
OF THE FRENCH REVOLUTION

The semiotic complexity of the commemorative stamp which, as I suggested at the beginning of this chapter, played both an iconic and an indexical role, is well illustrated by French stamps celebrating the Bicentenary of the French Revolution. This series set out systematically to transform the stamp, whose original function is indexical, into an icon. This is achieved by marginalising, as far as possible, all indexical elements. This is evident particularly in the chief indexical element of the stamp, the device *République française*, which is on at least ten occasions incorporated vertically, like a border, to the left or right of the main image. This point has already been noted in the context of the latest French definitive stamp, Briat's *Marianne* design, which, of all the stamps short listed in the Philexfrance competition in 1989, was the only one to place the identifying device vertically. The functional indicator *Postes* is similarly aligned on the vertical axis set up by the tricolour shading of the stamp's surface. In this way, symbols and indices are incorporated into what is an essentially iconic scheme.

This has often, of course, been the case with French commemorative stamps. What is striking about the various Bicentenary series is the systematic iconisation of the sign. This development is moreover evident on two levels; within each stamp and on the level of individual sets which are almost always presented in *se tenant* blocks or even as indivisible or with decorative vignettes attached (plates XIII and XIV). On the level of the individual stamp, one notices a tendency for certain iconic elements to be incorporated in further iconic motifs, creating the effect of a kind of iconic *mise en abîme*. In the *Personnages célèbres de la Révolution* (first series, plate XIII), for example, a scene from the life of each historical figure is framed by the profile of *Marianne* decked out in Phrygian bonnet with revolutionary rosette. In turn this profile is itself delineated with three bands of colour – the red, white and blue of the *Tricolore*. We thus see a visual image constructed on three levels of iconic development. The functional or indexical elements of the stamp – its face value plus surcharge, the country's name and the title of the scene illustrated in the stamp – are all inscribed in a somewhat jumbled way on the right hand side of the stamp. In this way, the exemplary icon of France – the profile of *Marianne* – opens like a Chinese box to display the wealth of its iconography and its historical pertinence. In the Philexfrance stamps issued in 1987 and 1988, mentioned above (figs 25 and 26), these elements are juxtaposed rather than integrated into the same design.

Above all, however, it is on the level of sets or on that of the stamp plus explicatory or decorative vignette that the iconic tendencies of the French Bicentenary stamps are most evident. Let me first of all point out the various ways in which iconographic elements are incorporated into the external framework of the stamps: stamp with *se tenant* vignette (Philexfrance, 1987, fig 25); stamp with indivisible vignette (Philexfrance 1988, fig 26); *se tenant* block of six stamps sold as a *carnet* with vignette (*Personnages de la Révolution*, first series, 1989, plate XIII); *se tenant* block of four stamps with decorative border surrounding (*Personnages de la Révolution*, second series, 1989, plate XIII); *se tenant* and indivisible blocks of four stamps with vignette (*Déclaration des droits de l'homme*, 1989, plate XIV).

This use of *se tenant* or indivisible blocks of stamps manifests a desire to reproduce as far as possible the graphic and the semantic content of the semiotic elements used, be they text, engraving or painting. What is offered, in effect, is a complete and as far as possible authentic documentation of the Revolutionary period, like that which one might find in a well-illustrated and apparently objective history textbook. It is for this reason that, as far as possible, authentic documents and engravings from the 1780s and 1790s have been adapted. Thus, in the series celebrating the Declaration of the Rights of Man, the text of the first seventeen articles has been spread across four stamps which are read as if they were the original text (plate XIV). The divisions marked by the stamps' perforations and again by the discreet vertical insertion of the device *République française*, are scarcely noticed by the stamp enthusiast who is struck by the unusual continuity of the text as it spreads across the stamps and the repetition of the *fasces* motif reproduced, as on many Bicentenary stamps, in the revolutionary colours. Perhaps even more appealing to collectors is the second series of *Personnages de la Révolution* (plate XIII) in which the *mise en abîme* effect of the first is applied to a *se tenant* block of stamps. Here the exploits of Madame Roland, Camille Desmoulins, Condorcet and Kellerman, individually illustrated in the four stamps, are elaborated iconographically by the decorative border framing the block. Pikes swathed in Tricolours, topped by the Phrygian bonnet and the revolutionary rosette, are picked out in the same colours as the stamps themselves – red, white, blue and green; the Tricolour crowned with laurels further binds together internal and external iconographic elements. It is through such icons that the sacred texts and images of democratic and revolutionary France are proclaimed, conventional indices being relatively marginalised. These stamps were conceived principally for collectors, a fact underlined by Philexfrance's close co-operation in their design and launch. Elements of national culture are packaged and marketed to consumers as more or less autonomous icons to be collected as objects.

Marketing aside, what is the ideological function of the iconic pleonasms that are evident throughout French Bicentenary stamp issues? First, it seems that the superabundance of icons offered reinforces the desired message (I shall return in a moment to the content of this 'message') without articulating it too clearly or literally. It is for this reason that images predominate over text – except where the text is itself a sacred icon of the nation. An attempt has therefore been made to present positive and attractive images of the French Revolution and to avoid the more disturbing ambiguities, horrors or disasters. In this respect, it is as interesting to note the images of the French Revolution that have been avoided as those that have been promoted; there are no or very few scenes of violence (as depicted in many contemporary prints, such as the Dutch vignette illustrated in fig 33), no evocation of the guillotine, of scenes of the Terror or even of the storming of the Bastille. The unfortunate Louis XVI is absent from the scene except in the stamp devoted to Drouet (in the first *Personnages célèbres de la Révolution* series, plate XIII) where he is glimpsed in the background as he tries to make his escape from France with Marie-Antoinette. There are no battle scenes (despite the presence of Kellerman in the second *Personnages célèbres* series) except for the *Journée des tuiles* at Grenoble (plate XV), reproduced after a nineteenth-century painting, which reduces considerably the violence of the scene. What is proposed, is a plethora of 'documents' and of engravings; in other words, the Bicentenary propaganda is pursued rather as it was at the time, using emblems and caricatures, except that in 1989 the revolutionary pikes are purely symbolic and visual images have as for the most part been transformed by art and consequently tamed in the process. The Bicentenary stamps, like modern French politicians, speak essentially the language of rhetorical or theatrical gestures. They prefer conventions or declarations, allegorical representations which draw general and relatively uncritical assent. Like the propaganda of the revolutionary period itself, the stamps illustrate the various ways in which the ideological image is constructed, in particular through a synthesis of iconographical elements (logos, emblems, coats of arms) and the reduction of textual elements to a strict minimum.

This emphasis on the icon, rather than the indexical function of the stamp, allows the latter, as a sign, to be manipulated in such a way that an ideological message may be proposed. However, although there is a degree of synchronisation between image and reader – enough to make the signifying process work – this does not necessarily prevent perception of the problematic nature of sign functions. The process is further complicated by the fact that although the indexical function of the stamp as sign is in effect hijacked by the iconic elements, the semiotic interference that ensues to a certain extent causes the indexical function of the stamp to temper iconic ambitions. *Marianne* indicates France the geographical country as well as representing the ideological construct that is the French republic.

Notes

1   The success of the French *Ceres* design is attested to not only by its longevity in France, but also by its adaptation during the nineteenth century by the stamps of other European countries including Greece, Norway and Romania. See William Finlay, *An Illustrated History of Stamp Design*, Peter Lowe, London 1974, pp30-31.

2   *Mercure* is traditionally associated with *Commerce*, appearing on the back of a Deputies' medal at the time of Louis-Philippe (1830-48) where it accompanies *Liberté* and various other allegorical figures, including *Agriculture* (a female figure carrying sheaves of wheat), as well as in Sage's *Paix et commerce* stamp of 1876-1900.

3   *Marianne's* evolution as an emblem of Liberty, of Republicanism and of France is explored by Maurice Aghulon in his classic studies *Marianne au combat: l'imagerie et la symbolique rébublicaines de 1879 à 1800*, Flammarion, Paris 1979 (English translation, Cambridge University Press, 1981) and *Marianne au pouvoir: l'imagerie et la symbolique républicaines de 1880 à 1914*, Flammarion, Paris, 1989. See also Maurice Aghulon and Pierre Bonte, *Marianne: les visages de la République*, Gallimard, Paris 1992, Coll Découvertes, and David Scott, 'National Icons: the Semiotics of the French Stamp', *French Cultural Studies III*, 1992, pp215-33.

4   The fiftieth anniversary of Dulac's *Marianne* was celebrated in 1994 by the stamp, engraved by Jumelet, illustrated in fig 31.

5   In 1940, a joint British and French stamp, for which essays were designed by Edmund Dulac and by Henri Cheffer, both of whom, as we saw, subsequently created stamps based on the *Marianne* theme, was planned to show Anglo-French solidarity in the face of the Nazi menace. In Dulac's design, *Marianne* and *Britannia's* heads are seen together in profile. The project was later dropped in 1940 when Germany invaded France. See the *British Philatelic Journal*, VIII no 8, 1971, pp3-5 and XXV, no 4 (1987), pp80-83.

AVANT-GARDE STAMP DESIGN
The Dutch Post Office

The Dutch, along with the Swiss, have one of the strongest design traditions of any small European country, one that has had an impact far beyond its own borders.[1] The Dutch were perhaps the first to relate developments in stamp design to the larger world of industrial creation, architecture, graphics and visual awareness in general. In a sense, therefore, a study of their stamps from the 1920s onwards is more or less a study of modern graphic design.

1

2

This chapter, in investigating stamp design in the Netherlands, will focus on two periods. The first, from the 1920s until just after the Second World War, will explore the relationship between design theory and the practice of artists and graphic designers as it related both to De Stijl and other modernist movements, and to the older Dutch graphic arts tradition. The second will show how many of the issues raised by Dutch philatelic design in the 1920s and 1930s have again been confronted in stamps issued by the Netherlands from the 1960s. The aim will be to show how the different design priorities emerging from the historic and modern traditions in the earlier part of this century, raise issues that are fundamental to an assessment of the status of the philatelic image; issues that continue to influence stamp design today, not only in the Netherlands, but also elsewhere in Europe and the world.

As a theoretical basis for the analysis that follows, I shall continue to use the Peircian terminology – icon, index, symbol – introduced at the beginning of this study, especially since Dutch stamps offer an exemplary illustration of the semiotic process as Peirce describes it. Jan van Krimpen's definitive set, used from 1946 to 1973, with its simple calligraphic face values and name of country, perfectly exemplifies the indexical function (fig 1). Meanwhile, the iconic function is illustrated well in Sem Harz's classic adaptation of the Penny Black formula to the Dutch stamp in his 1947 series (fig 2). Finally, the tension between indexical and iconic functions in the commemorative stamp can be seen in a number of Dutch issues.[2]

A discussion of the philatelic status of the stamp in a *design* context is bound to focus on the two different iconic functions it can fulfil. This is because the official or indexical function of the national icon (such as the head of state) will obviously lend itself much less to design initiative than icons connected with broader commemorative functions. As a result of this, in many instances (Dutch practice being just one of these), the distinct functions of the definitive and the commemorative stamp have tended to find expression in different formats and in a different approach to the design of the stamp.[3] The status of the stamp as an official document, emitted by a royal or government agency, has mostly been guarded jealously, particularly in European stamps, with the result that, even to the present day, definitive stamps are more sober and formal in their design. Adopting a smaller, standardised format, they usually embody an official or national icon to enhance immediate recognition of the state of their origin.

The commemorative stamp, on the other hand, has usually been allowed a greater variety of formats (square, oblong, triangular), a wider range of styles, with much more scope given to the designer to produce images appropriate to

Cees de Jong, Europa: Architecture, 1987, (Plate XX, vii), detail

the event or person commemorated. In this respect, it is more like a miniature poster except that it still has to fulfil the official functions of marking and identifying postage. Because of this, the commemorative stamp has a far wider range of iconic potential than the definitive stamp, whose central image must primarily express the state which issues it. This separation between definitive and commemorative functions only began to become clear in the early years of the twentieth century. Indeed, until the 1920s, most stamps – even the early commemoratives – adopted the simple and effective formula invented by Sir Roland Hill in 1840 for the British 'Penny Black', using the smaller definitive format (approximately 250 x 200 mm) as a framework for the display of national icon or name of country, plus face value. I think it is no accident that a realisation of the wider design scope of the stamp was made at a time in Europe (the 1920s) when the potential of design was being reassessed radically.

(I) THE 1920-1940S PERIOD

In no country was philatelic design being more radically reassessed than in the Netherlands. From 1920, Jean-François van Royen (1878-1942) was the General Secretary of the national postal and telecommunications service (PTT), a man gifted with not only exceptional artistic taste but also with a deep knowledge of typography and design. Van Royen had joined the PTT as a humble clerical assistant in 1904 and during his rise through the ranks was progressively to influence the PTT's design policy in an increasingly wide and profound manner. He was in a position to do this thanks to his activities outside the PTT, which included private publishing, a practical as well as aesthetic interest in typography and printing, and, above all, his involvement in the Netherlands Association for Crafts and Industrial Art, the VANK, of which he became chairman in 1922.[4] The VANK was formed in 1904 to promote the development of crafts, industrial arts and design, and in 1915 an advisory board was set up which offered its services to government departments undertaking projects involving design. Van Royen was the secretary to the board and through this position was able to make recommendations to official organisations including his own, the PTT. Van Royen was commemorated on one of the Summer stamps of 1947, designed by Mrs E Reitsma-Valença (fig 3).

3

4

Possible new directions in Dutch stamp design in the 1920s were also a function of the emergence at this time of the avant-garde movement in Dutch art and design. As G Forde has suggested:

> the Dutch avant-garde emerged from two seemingly irreconcilable trends which characterised Dutch art and design before and during the war. The first of these was an insistence on decoration and eclecticism and was most evident in the Amsterdam school; the second was an idealisation of purity and geometric abstraction in the loose grouping of artists, designers and architects called De Stijl.[5]

This dual tradition is seen clearly in the development of Dutch stamp design from the 1920s which, under the influence of Van Royen, drew on a range of artists and designers of unprecedented quality and variety. It is in this sense that a survey of Dutch philatelic design in the period from 1920 until just after the Second World War (Van Royen died in a concentration camp in 1942) offers remarkable insight into early modern graphic design. It also shows how different aspects of the design tradition are drawn on by philatelic designers, depending on the functions the stamp has to fulfil. In particular, the tension between the two central conceptions of the stamp – on the one hand seen as an official State document, on the other as a miniature commemorative poster – is often made clearly visible in the artistic and design solutions developed to deal with these differently perceived functions. Thus, on the whole, the older decorative, calligraphic tradition tended to be employed for definitive stamps and those celebrating traditional aspects of the national culture, while avant-garde models – exploiting the new typography, photo-montage, abstract and geometrical composition – were, thanks to Van Royen, increasingly used in the design of Dutch commemorative issues. It is also worth noting that those artists and designers influenced by De Stijl and other modern movements who worked for the PTT, shared with Van Royen a conception of the postage stamp as being just one aspect of a much larger design concept (including everything from posters and information leaflets to furniture design and architecture) which the stamp would reflect. This contrasted

5

6

7

8

with the traditional concept of the stamp as a representation of an integral, national idea, or of the state or monarch as perceived historically, relatively independent of changes in style and fashion. This tension is visible through Dutch stamp design from the 1920s to the present day.[6] Since the 1960s, in the Netherlands as in Britain too, it is the more radical and avant-garde design traditions that have increasingly held sway (see plate XX).

The Dutch artists commissioned to design stamps in the 1920s were largely drawn from that generation born between about 1860 and the 1880s who matured as artists at the time of the Arts and Crafts movement and who were thus always as much concerned with design as with more purely aesthetic matters. Nearly all of them were noted poster designers, dealing with an increasing number of commercial commissions, and with a strong leaning towards the decorative arts. The most famous of them was probably Jan Toorop (1858-1928) who, although born in Java (then part of the Dutch East Indies), moved to the Netherlands as a young man and trained as an artist at the Rijksakademie, Amsterdam. He also studied at the Brussels Academy and, in the 1880s, visited London, where he was strongly influenced by William Morris. By 1923, the time the Dutch PTT commissioned him to produce designs for commemorative stamps to promote the national Culture Fund, he was a well-established artist. The pair of stamps issued, a set of two in strikingly bold colours (fig 4, the 2c violet, the 10c orange), are distinctly Art Nouveau in style, displaying the strong linear tendencies and highly stylised forms also visible in Toorop's poster designs for Delft Salad Oil of about 1895 or the Association for the Promotion of Tourism of about 1900 (fig 5).

The work of Toorop's slightly younger contemporaries, Chris Lebeau (1878-1945), Jacob Jongert (1883-1942) and PAH Hofman (1885-1965), continues the Art Nouveau tradition, although their work of the 1920s was beginning to shed some of the decorative excess of this style and adopt more simplified, though still highly stylised, forms. The demands of the postage stamp's very restricted format obviously had an impact here and it is interesting to see how quickly these artists' philatelic designs, which initially tended towards a scaling down of the poster image, turned to a more radical reassessment of the graphic scope of the postage stamp format. This is particularly true of the work of Hofman and Lebeau.[7]

Joris Johannes Christiaan (Chris) Lebeau, born in Amsterdam in 1878, was a graphic designer and decorative artist who produced textiles, glass and ceramics as well as printing, poster and stamp designs. In addition to studying at the Quellinusschool (1892-95) and the Rijksschool voor Kunstnijverheid (1895-99), Lebeau also took drawing lessons from Karel Petrus Cornelis de Bazel (1869-1923) who, at the instigation of Van Royen, had designed an innovative stamp commemorating the 1913 centenary of Dutch independence (plate XVI, i). Lebeau's method as a stamp designer seems to have been to take the striking symmetrical motifs that he had developed as a poster designer – as in the memorable images he created for the theatre, see *Hamlet*, 1914 (fig 6) – and to scale them down and simplify them. One can see, for example, how the wing motif launched in his first set of stamps, the *Air* series of 1921 (fig 7), is simplified and refined to become the carrier pigeon in 1924 that was to be retained as the image on Dutch lower-value definitive stamps for the next twenty years (fig 8). This was one of the first stamps to be produced in the Netherlands by the offset-litho process, with its bright colour and bold typography, was the first Dutch stamp that was truly modern in appearance. The break with the past that it marks is made all the clearer by a comparison with the higher-value definitive series issued at the same time (fig 9). The latter, the work of Jan Veth, could have been designed seventy years earlier, its royal profile, decorative border, classic typography and engraved image linking it directly to stamps of the Victorian era and of an older Dutch design tradition. Lebeau's next set of stamps, an *Air* series of 1928 commemorating Koppen and Van der Hoop, pioneers of Dutch postal aviation (fig 10), continues the modern idiom, though the lithographic process used here and the extensive use of 'engraved' lines, produce a less contemporary effect than the offset image of the 1924 set.

10

9

The transformation of Dutch postage stamp design from an Art Nouveau to a contemporary idiom is also well illustrated by the philatelic work of PAH Hofman. Like Lebeau, Hofman was an artist of many interests and skills, a painter, printmaker and craftsman, producing wall paintings, stained glass, posters and book covers as well as stamp designs. His first stamps, commemorating the Dutch Lifeboat Centenary in 1924 (fig 11), propose images in which, as they do in his posters of this period (fig 12), Art Nouveau arabesques hold sway over the object in question (lifeboat, yacht in distress). Although this can be expressive – in the 2c stamp, the yacht is almost submerged beneath the decorative arabesques of the waves – it does not necessarily lead to clear overall design; the face value and commemorative dates take up so much space that there is no room left for the name of the country! The replacement of the arabesque by the diagonal and the more effective integration of word and image, is visible both in Hofman's later poster and stamp designs. For example, his poster for the Annual Industries Fair, Utrecht, 1930 (fig 13) has *Mercury* striding across a contemporary industrial landscape, whose dynamism is expressed by a lightning-flash zigzag with which both the lettering and *Mercury's* body are synchronised. Similarly, Hofman's Peace propaganda stamp of 1933 (fig 14) is exemplary in its modernity, the coherent simplified design of the central motif being perfectly encapsulated in the stamp format.[8] A similarly radical change in graphic style between 1920 and 1930 is visible in the work of Jacob Jongert, painter, graphic designer and director of advertising for Van Nelle of Rotterdam from 1923 to 1940. The style changed from the Art Nouveau complexity of his 1920 Van Nelle tobacco poster – in which *Nicotiana* flowers transform themselves into tobacco smoke, which in turn becomes lettering (fig 15) – to the geometric simplicity of the 1930 poster for Van Nelle Tea and Coffee (fig 16). Jongert's stamp for the 1929 *Air* set (fig 17) has not yet achieved the simplicity of his later poster designs, being based on an engraving of a *Mercury* that is decorative and mythological rather than modern and functional in style.

12

It was not until the early 1930s that this modern functional style, perfected by the artists and designers associated with De Stijl, was to appear on Dutch postage stamps. The artists who produced these designs, a generation younger than Jongert and Lebeau, were less influenced by Art Nouveau than by *De Stijl* whose launch in 1917 by Theo van Doesburg was followed in the 1920s by an intense period of experiment and discussion among the major figures associated with it – Bart van der Leck, Piet Mondrian, Gerrit Rietveld, Vilmos Huszar and Van Doesburg himself. By 1931, when Van Doesburg died and *De Stijl* ceased to be, the ideas generated had filtered into the work of artists, architects and designers peripheral to the movement and are exemplified in the stamp designs of Piet Zwart (1885-1977), Gerard Kiljan (1891-1968) and Paul Schuitema (1897-1973).

Although the progressive functionalism promoted by *De Stijl* was already manifesting itself in the 1920s in the advertising design of commercial companies (as noted above in the context of Jongert's posters for Van Nelle of 1930), it was nevertheless a bold and controversial step on Van Royen's part to commission avant-garde artists to design posters, booklets and postage stamps for a government agency, the PTT. The reaction was predictably hostile but Van Royen persisted, with the

13

10

11

14

17

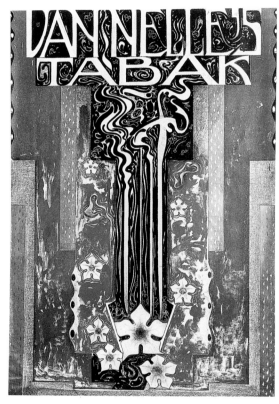

15

result that for a brief period in the 1930s, the Netherlands produced stamps that were fifty years ahead of those of the rest of the world. These stamps reflected the design philosophy of De Stijl in their functionalism; the direct confrontation of the image (mostly reproduced photographically); their use of simplified, sanserif typefaces and of diagonals as well as horizontals and verticals in relation to the alignment of both image and lettering; their superimposition of text and image using montage, and their functional use of colour (different motifs in the design distinguished by hue as much as by other elements). Their aim in this was to stress the link between the symbolic elements of the philatelic sign (text, typography) and the icons (photographic or other images), thus increasing the immediacy and semiotic efficiency of the stamp.

Piet Zwart's extensive skills in modern typography and photomontage, enabled him to meet the challenge of stamp design in a startlingly original way.[9] His *Wilhelmina* stamps of 1931 (fig 19), for example, juxtapose a photograph of the monarch (the first time a royal head ever appeared in this medium on a stamp) with industrial scenes. The Queen's head in a circle at the lower part of the stamp is balanced by name of the country and face value of the stamp printed in contrasting colour (red) at the top. Homage was paid to this formula fifty years later in 1980 with a PTT design commemorating Beatrix's accession to the throne (fig 18). In the *Air* version of Zwart's stamp (fig 20), the typography is aligned diagonally to synchronise with the banking aircraft in the upper part of the image. The same year, he produced even more radically functional designs (one is shown in fig 21) to commemorate the Gouda Church restoration fund, photo-montages in which a diagonally positioned rhombus (photographs of interior and exterior of the church) is juxtaposed with a circular motif in which working craftsmen are shown. The commemorative text is aligned with and overlaps the rhombus, the country's name, in small print, being relegated to the top left of the stamp. More striking still were his designs submitted, but rejected, for a 1½ c stamp. These designs were purely typographic – and it was half a century before such a stamp actually appeared – reflecting his practice as poster artist at the time (figs 22-23). Zwart clarified his views about the strictly functional nature of philatelic design in 1939 when he stated:

> The postage stamp is a document of the times. It does not primarily pose an aesthetic problem and has nothing in common with a painting. The truly authentic postage stamp is one which displays the attributes of the period from which it comes, constitutes a synthesis of its originating idea and which is produced using contemporary technological methods. Any other basis is false and unworthy. Moreover, the stamp in use is part of a larger whole, the postal article, and thereby loses its independence. The conventional format, namely a symmetrical image along a vertical axis (in some cases horizontal), lends the stamp an autonomy which is not its due. Consequently, in my stamps I have adopted a dynamic composition, and have made corresponding use of the photographic and photo-technical reproduction methods so representative of our time. Whether the results are considered beautiful or ugly is of less importance.[10]

The relationship between typography and photographic image explored by Gerard Kiljan in his posters and booklets (fig 24) is also adapted to the *Kinderzegels* stamp issue of 1931 (fig 25, plate XVI). Child Welfare stamps, issued on an annual basis in the Netherlands since 1924, had until this time proposed conservative, primarily decorative images of children, of provincial coats of arms or of famous Dutchman.[11] In contrast, Kiljan's photographic images of clearly disabled children in bold colour against a white background, were revolutionary in their realism

een kleine keuze uit onze lettercollectie

INTERNATIONALE
TENTOONSTELLING
OP FILMGEBIED

ITF

FILM

14 APRIL
15 MEI
1928 GROOTE KONINKLIJKE
BAZAR ZEESTRAAT 82
DEN HAAG

22 - 23
24 - 26

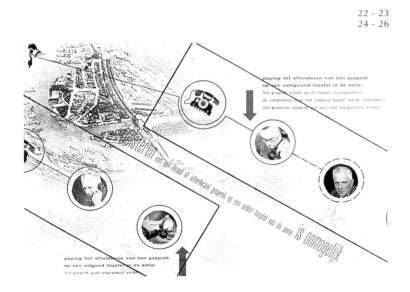

CENTRALE BOND

30 000

TRANSPORTARBEIDERS

16

18

19

20

21

25

27

28

and directness. Their impact is enhanced by the way the human figures depicted are photo-montaged in such a way that they extend beyond the colour boundary of the image, reaching, as it were, out of the stamp towards the viewer. The oblique typography of the commemorative text is deliberately out of synchronisation with the rest of the typographic elements, enhancing the feeling of unease created by the image.

Like Zwart, Paul Schuitema was an architect and photographer, a typographical designer and also a film-maker, who, like Zwart, was influenced by El Lissitsky and Russian constructivism as well as by *De Stijl*. When he wrote the following in *Neue Grafik* in 1926, he summarises his own practice and that of Zwart and Kiljan as stamp designers:

It was essential that our designs should be taut and arresting. The first and most important colour to use was red. Blue and yellow came later. We always used primary colours, never mixtures. We favoured sanserif type: condensed and spaced, bold and light. These were the principles on which we worked. Photomontage was equally important to us. We applied the photograph freely to the flat rectangular surface, never making use of proportion or of drawing for that would have been too much like painting. If we drew we abstracted or simplified as much as possible and went straight for the objective without any romantic trimmings'.[12]

Schuitema's *Tourist Propaganda* stamps issued in 1932 (fig 27, plate XVI) are an ideal illustration of this theory. Four stamps in single colours (green, black, red, blue) propose photomontages that are both bold and subtle; in each case, two images on different scales (windmill and dyke, historic building and modern streets, bridge and viaduct, tulips and fields) are juxtaposed at different angles, the overall image nevertheless creating a remarkable effect of unity. Clear, bold typography in white and black is superimposed on the montage, the ANVV acronym of the Dutch National Tourist Board being disposed vertically along the left border. No frills, no decoration but an image that is both functional and alluring. In many ways, Schuitema's stamps are the most successful of the avant-garde series in that although they could easily be scaled up to work as posters (the stamps appeared much enlarged on advertisements) they also work scaled down to the stamp format with a typography better adjusted in both boldness and scale. An example of Schuitema's work as a poster designer can be seen in fig 26. One feels with Zwart's and Kiljan's designs, especially given the small format of the latter, that the image has suffered from reduction in scale and from typefaces that are swamped by their white backgrounds.

Thus, issues are raised regarding both the wider relevance to the discussion of philatelic design and the relative unpopularity of Zwart's and Kiljan's designs in the 1930s. The crux of the problem is that of legibility and scale. Although, in principle, legibility formed a vital part of De Stijl design theory, for some graphic artists it was not necessarily a priority. Surprise, provocation, and novelty were also primary aims, ones that betray the impact of Dada, constructivist and of the contemporary movements on the development of the Dutch avant-garde.[13] Equally important were Functionalism and simplicity. The adoption by Zwart and some De Stijl designers, under the influence of Albers and Bayer at the Bauhaus, of a uniquely lower-case alphabet was a logical move from a design point of view but one not readily appreciated by the consumer of the printed text, who was accustomed to capitalisation as a means of pinpointing important parts of the linguistic message.

Although lower case typography did not appear on a Dutch stamp until 1947 (fig 28), Zwart and Kiljan's typeface is very light and simplified. For the unsophisticated eyes of the majority of users in the early 1930s, the typeface, combined with the large areas of white, seemed almost invisible. Traditional stamp design, on the other hand, with its ultra-clear lettering, its distinctive non-primary colours, its heavily-engraved image and its focus on a central, easily identifiable visual icon, was much more legible, even at the reduced scale of the definitive format. It is here that scale plays a vital role. Kiljan and Zwart's designs are essentially poster images reduced to stamp format, and consequently they lose some of their legibility in the process. It has only been with the progressive visual education of the public in the sixties and seventies (through television and other media) along with the technical advances in photogravure and other printing processes, that stamps have been able to use the sophisticated design techniques introduced by artists at the time of the Bauhaus and *De Stijl*. In the later thirties and through the war years and beyond, Dutch stamp design tended to return to more conventional design formulas, or to adopt a less flagrantly radical approach to design.

This does not mean that Dutch stamp designers ceased to respond to the challenges of the modern world but rather that, for a time, they shifted the emphasis back to perfecting the graphic legibility of their art and to responding to the demands of modern themes. The aeroplane, a signifier of modernity already from Apollinaire's time, inevitably posed a challenge to stamp designers (airmail services became increasingly widespread from the 1920s), and many leading Dutch stamp designers from Lebeau and Jongert through Zwart and Escher to Van Dobbenburgh leapt at the opportunity. Aart van Dobbenburgh, born in 1899, was a painter and graphic artist, studied at the various Amsterdam schools, was taught drawing by De Bazel, and was the first Dutchman after Zwart to create a modern image of the aircraft in the postage stamp framework. In his Airmail design of 1933 (fig 29), he cleverly builds the triangular profile of the stamp round the vertical axis of the aircraft propeller, with all textual elements in distinct block capitals incorporated into the triangular framework. By doing so, he achieves a completely legible and functional design. In his next airmail stamp in 1938 (fig 30), Van Dobbenburgh adopts a more expressionist approach, one not unrelated to some of his posters of the mid-1930s, such as *De Drinker* of 1935. Here, the stamp, which represents not an aircraft but a crow, is a photo reproduction of a painting and depends for its effect upon the poignant image of the bird, the beautiful dark blues and the excellent way in which the lettering has been added to the pictorial design. This stamp was so successful it was re-released in 1953 with a 25c face value.

29

30

31

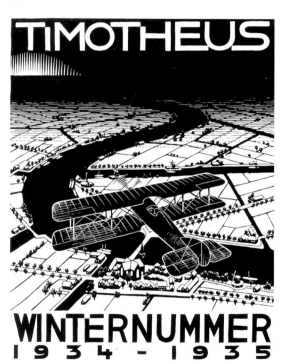

32

33

34a   34b

35   36

37

Even more original than Van Dobbenburgh's stamp design was that created by his contemporary MC Escher (1898-1972) for the Air Fund in 1935 (fig 31). Escher's work as an artist scarcely needs any introduction – his extraordinary woodcuts and lithographs of pictorial *mises en abîme* and other visual conundrums gained him an international reputation from the mid-1930s. Produced by photogravure, the 1935 stamp is not entirely typical of Escher, although the theme had been explored by Escher in design for the magazine *Timotheus* the year before (fig 32). What is typically Escher about the 1935 stamp is the idiosyncratic but effective way that visual elements work together to produce an image of almost hallucinatory clarity. First, the flat surface of the stamp is criss-crossed with longitudinal and latitudinal lines, which create the illusion of the Earth's curvature. These are superimposed on the map of the Netherlands, though there is obviously no direct relationship between the two, the country being too small to figure within the scheme of global curvature instituted by the lines. However, the sense of the country being part of the earth's surface is enhanced by the addition of the profiles or shadows of a squadron of planes flying overhead, the superimposition of the name of the country on its image within the stamp strengthening the illusion that the country is being viewed both as part of the surface of the globe and as a map. By including the country's name (an indexical function of the sign) within the commemorative frame (the iconic aspect of the sign) Escher has maximised the semiotic efficiency of the stamp image. Moving the textual elements to its borders clarifies the stamp's commemorative function and further enhances the visual impact of the main image.[14] A similarly graphic effect is created by Escher in a design completed in 1932, but in the event not used, for a peace stamp (fig 33).

The relationship between Escher's work as an artist and his philatelic designs is much closer in his next stamps, issued in 1949 to commemorate the 75th anniversary of the Universal Postal Union, a set that coincided with a major exhibition of Escher's work at the Boymans-Van Beuningen Museum in Rotterdam. There are two versions of the UPU design, one (fig 34a) figuring on the stamp issued in the Netherlands, the other (fig 34b) in the two Dutch colonies of Surinam and Dutch Antilles. The focus of both designs is a globe on which postal horns interlock in an intricate but rhythmic manner. In a sense, the colonial stamp is the more effective in that the global motif, which in this version is larger, seems to float in three-dimensional space, announcing its intention at any moment to spin out of the stamp, thus creating the optical illusion so characteristic of Escher's work.

If Escher was an idiosyncratic but inspired choice as a stamp designer, so too was Pijke Koch (1901-91), who designed stamps for the Netherlands and its colonies over a period of twenty years. Koch was a 'magic realist' painter who established his reputation in the Low Countries in the 1930s, and later internationally. His stamps are strongly figurative in content and are most successful when they incorporate lettering by Jan van Krimpen (1892-1958), the noted Dutch calligrapher and engraver. Koch's *Boy Scout Jamboree* designs of 1937, owing principally to their weak lettering, compare unfavourably with those designed with Van Krimpen later the same year for the *Child Welfare* series (fig 35). Equally accomplished, is the *Coronation Jubilee* set produced by these designers in 1938 (fig 36), in which a fine portrait of Wilhelmina, framed in elegant lettering, establishes a format for royal or other official commemorative stamps that was successfully applied over subsequent decades, principally by Sem Hartz (born in 1912). More controversial was Koch's *Old Germanic Symbols* set, issued in 1943 (fig 37, plate XVII). These were particularly beautiful designs, but are in effect propaganda for the Germans who occupied the Netherlands from 1940 to 1945.

In the immediate post-war period, Dutch stamps continued to uphold an extremely high level of graphic design, both in relation to lettering – see Van Krimpen's new numeral definitives, issued in 1946 (fig 1, plate XVII), which graced Dutch mail for a quarter of a century – and to the figurative image. Sem Hartz, WZ Van Dijk, CL Mechelse and Van Krimpen's *Summer* stamps of 1948 (fig 38, plate XVII) continued rather magisterially in the formula established by Koch and Van Krimpen in 1938, this time incorporating architectural images. It was against stamps such as these, timeless in their clarity, elegance and formal perfection that the more innovative designs of a new generation of designers of the 1960s would be measured (see also the issues reproduced on plate XVIII and Hartz's *Erasmus* commemorative of 1969, fig 39).

The finest tribute to the innovative stamp design in the Netherlands in the 1920s and 1930s has undoubtedly been made by Dutch stamps of the 1970s and 1980s. Throughout the 1950s and 1960s Dutch stamp design was second to none with Sem Harz's pupil Paul Wetselaar producing some of the most attractive stamps ever issued by the Netherlands and its colonies (fig 40 and plate XIX). However, design continued to follow the patterns established by Koch, Hartz and Van Krimpen in the 1930s and 1940s. From the early 1960s there was a marked return to functionalism and the exploitation of contemporary technologies, in particular computer-aided graphics and sophisticated colour separation.[15] Here, one might pinpoint Otto Treumann's *Telephone* series of 1962 (fig 41) and Wim Crouwel's *Paris Postal Conference Centenary* of 1963 (fig 42) as key developments. Crouwel's numerical definitives of 1976 (fig 43), replacing the Van Krimpen series, confirm this trend and reflect the cool graphic style Crouwel had developed in his poster designs, many of which were purely typographical (fig 44). The reduced concern with the prevention of forgeries gave stamp designers new freedom which, coupled with a more sophisticated and visually tolerant public, led them to experiment once again with the iconic and message-bearing potential of the stamp as a medium.[16]

38

39

40

41

42

43

44

(II) DUTCH STAMP DESIGN FROM THE 1960s

Dutch philatelic designers from the 1960s onwards have submitted the postage stamp to radical investigation from both a concept and a design point of view. This investigation has not taken the form of modish tinkering with the geometry of the stamp format (most of the most daring designs to appear in the Netherlands over the last thirty years adopt the standard commemorative rectangle) but rather an exploration of the internal conventions of stamp design. Considerations include: the degree to which legibility is a priority, in relation both to image and typography (a question that has implications both for the status and clarity of typography and the role of icons in expressing the message of the stamp); the relationship between stamp format, perforation and image frame and the extent to which the graphic medium itself can become the chief interest of a given design; the scope of photomontage; the role of new media, including computer graphics; and the ability of the stamp to exploit the strip cartoon, newspaper leader, poster, and other graphic formats in the interest of communicating the philatelic message. In exploring questions such as these, this section will show once again how richly stamps illustrate fundamental design and semiotic issues.

TYPOGRAPHY

For the stamp designer, typography can fulfil both iconic and symbolic functions in relaying the philatelic message. This double function is symptomatic of two deep but contradictory tendencies of typography more generally, especially as it has been conceived in the twentieth century. For traditionalists, the role of typography is to promote the transparency of conventional linguistic symbols, the legibility of the text. For Beatrice Warde, for example, as for Dutch contemporaries like Jan van Krimpen, 'Printing Should be Invisible'.[17] One should not notice the form of the letters one is reading, however beautiful, since their role is to transmit the contents of the message they dutifully bear. For many typographers of the avant-garde and after, however, the typographic symbol should as far as possible transform itself into an icon, into a visible and tangible presence, even at the risk of undermining the textual message to which it gives body. For Warde, typographers of this persuasion, such as Piet Zwart or Paul Schuitema, are 'Stunt typographers', who play with letters without respecting the transparency of the message they are bound to communicate.

Warde's position, if sympathetic to those exasperated by illegibility, is nonetheless questionable. For it presupposes that any message is integral and complete *before* it becomes the subject of mediation through the chosen sign system of communication. However, as Marshall McLuhan and others have made clear since the 1950s, medium plays a determining role in the content as well as the form of the message. This is shown, as we shall see, by many Dutch stamps designed over the last thirty years. But even modern classic typographers such as Jan van Krimpen and Sem Hartz, while maintaining a fundamental commitment to legibility, nevertheless allow aspects of the typographic medium itself to become a major part of the pleasure enjoyed by the viewer, if not part of the message of the stamp. Thus in Van Krimpen's design for the 90th anniversary of the Dutch Red Cross, the rhythm created by the triple repetition of the elongated '7', becomes a visual motif, in a sense an icon, almost as important as the Red Cross itself (fig 45).

45

46

47

48

49

50

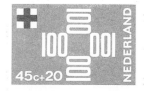

Rik Comello, design commemorating the Dutch Salvation Army, 1987, detail

51

52

53

54

55

The work of designers such as Van Krimpen and Van Stek in Dutch stamps after the Second World War also betrays a certain debt to the conventions of calligraphy, of which cursive strokes, scrolls and other extensions to letter forms are an integral part, contributing much to the beauty of the forms and the pleasure of reading (fig 46). The rich visual potential of typographic and calligraphic forms makes possible the purely typographic stamp, as in Van Krimpen's famous numerals set of 1946 (fig 1) and Sem Hartz's design of twenty years later (fig 47). The expressive 'message' stamps such as these communicate may be read as that of authentic ancient documents, royal seals or signatures, and the prestige of an art that has mastered epigraphic inscription in a manner immune to counterfeit.

The expressive potential of typography is explored more variously, radically and systematically by Dutch artists in the avant-garde tradition who draw their inspiration from the experiments of the De Stijl and Bauhaus groups in the 1920s and 1930s, and from developments in modern media and technology. For typographers of this sort, when the conventional symbols become iconic, it becomes more visible, more sensual, more opaque. It communicates to the reader, who is at first appealed to as a viewer, by emphasising its physical presence as a letter. This is shown, for example, in Jurriaan Schrofer's purely typographical stamp designed in 1969 to commemorate the IAO (fig 48, plate XIX). As in a concrete poem, the message of this stamp is read primarily as a typographic pattern, only deciphered secondarily as a series of letters that make sense as a text. In M Olijff's stamp commemorating the 30th anniversary of Benelux in 1974 (fig 49), the structure of the acronym BENELUX is deconstructed into three typographical constituents, 'BE' 'NE' 'LUX', the central 'NE' being aligned with the beginning of the word NEDERLAND, from which it originates. In this way, Olijff is able to link ingeniously the stamp's commemorative message (BENELUX) with its definitive message (NEDERLAND).

Symbolic signs can also take on an iconic dimension when they are used as elements in a visual design. In three of the five stamps designed to commemorate the centenary of the Red Cross in 1967, Wim van Stek uses purely typographical elements – numbers or letters – to construct the central cross motif (fig 50). In this way, typographical elements operate both as icons (proposing three different forms of the red cross) and as constituents in the stamp's symbolic or textual message. The idea of centenary (100), the anniversary dates (1867-1967) and the initials of the Dutch Red Cross organisation (NRK: Nederlandse Rode-Kruis) are thus interwoven.

In Gerrit Noordzij's stamp commemorating the fifth centenary of the *Bible of Delft* (fig 51), the dual function of typographical elements as both symbolic and iconic signs is activated in an even more comprehensive fashion. For Noordzij's stamp invites a reading on a number of different levels, each of which indicates precisely the typographical features used by the stamp in creating its message. First we are shown, literally, the letters or typographical characters, in this case *D* and *B*, that would have been used by the fifteenth-century type setter in constructing the words *Delftse* and *Bijbel*. They are exhibited on an extract from the *Bible*, this presentation inevitably obscuring part of the biblical text. Once again, legibility of the text is not the prime consideration but its presence as a significant object. (It can be noted that in the more traditional Dutch typographical stamp, the textual message is never obscured in any way). At a third level, we read through or behind the biblical text the letter '*a*', which is formed electronically. The function of this letter as icon is presumably to remind us of the distance separating modern electronic type setting from that used in 1477. For the reader/viewer/ philatelist to become fully aware of these different levels of reading, this stamp was accompanied by a vignette which explained its visual content and added details about its designer, its printer (Enschedé), the date of its issue, etc. In another purely typographical stamp, Noordzij commemorates the Dutch politician JR Thorbecke (1972, fig 52) simply by citing a quotation set in fine English copperplate script.

The way in which typography is able to incorporate iconic into its more normal symbolic functions is illustrated on a literal level by Gielijn Escher in his stamp of 1980 commemorating the centenary of the Free University Amsterdam (fig 53). Here, the typographical element – the numerical characters symbolising the idea of the centenary – are enlarged sufficiently to embrace or enclose the *visual* motifs or icons that they in part express in symbolic terms. Thus the first '0' becomes the circular frame of the portrait of the university's founder, Abraham Kuyper, while the second contains the university seal. Another way in which typographical elements are able to stress their iconic potential is by adopting an irregular disposition within the stamp frame. The dynamic diagonal forms, so much favoured by Dutch avant-garde typographers of the 1920s and 1930s, are frequently used in contemporary Dutch designs to this effect. In Marte Röling's *Korfbal* stamp of 1978 (fig 54) and in Otto Treumann's stamp commemorating elections to the European Parliament in 1979 (fig 55), the diagonal disposition is made even more expressive by the use of the Dutch national colours – red, white and blue. In both stamps, the large areas of blank space become activated by the diagonal imprint of the adjacent typography as fields of potential action; physical or sporting in the case of Röling's stamp, political in the case of Treumann's.

In relation to dynamic typography, another avant-garde practice much used by contemporary Dutch stamp designers is that of montage, or the superimposition of one or more type series. In a PTT design commemorating the 25th anniversary of European human rights, for example, the textual message of the stamp is superimposed on the large but shadowy characters '25 JAAR' (fig 56). In one of Anthon Beeke's set of three *Children's Rights* stamps (fig 57), two different typefaces – one conventional, one a reproduction of handwriting – are printed over a text, making a total of four different typefaces, each a different colour. Beeke's skill as a poster artist was particularly sought after for the theatre on account of the way he dramatises the relationship between the different typefaces used (fig 60). A similar palimpsest-like structure, again using typefaces of four different colours, is used by Karel Martens in his 1992 *Civil Code* stamp (fig 58). The way he superimposes the title of the code and, more daringly, the face-value (80c) of the stamp, on a fragment of the code text, makes him a worthy successor to Piet Zwart. Colour differentiation in relation to typography is also used effectively by Stephan Saaltink in his handsome Penal Code commemoration stamp of 1986 (fig 59) in which the stamp's message plus Van Strafrecht's dates are marked in yellow, while its definitive message is printed in purple.

SHIFTING THE IMAGE FRAME

One of the features that makes the work of avant-garde Dutch graphic artists of the 1920s and 1930s, such as Piet Zwart and Paul Schuitema, still seem modern today is the way they used the space of the format employed. In particular, they were among the first to realise that the rectangular frame of the poster, brochure, book-cover or leaflet need not determine the shape of the image or text for which it was the support. A carefully calculated discrepancy between format and image could create a certain dynamism which reminded the viewer/reader that he or she was looking at a piece of graphic art, not just an image or a message. The scope of such effects has been explored comprehensively by contemporary

57

58

59

60

Dutch postage stamp designers, the drastic reduction of scale demanded by the stamp format making the effect created seem all the more radical, especially within a genre in which legibility and regularity have been traditional priorities. The stamp's format is doubly defined, by both the perforation which marks it out as a stamp and the band of white that usually separates the image frame from the perforation. Both these features have been used by recent Dutch designers to destabilise as much as to order the configuration of the image within the stamp format.

61

The spatial as opposed to linear structuring that this implies is well illustrated in Rik Comello's *Dutch Salvation Army* design of 1987 (fig 61). Here, the image frame is not in synchronisation with the regular, rectangular perforated frame of the stamp, the white wedges in the left and top left sides of the stamp suggesting that the collage of images that fills most of the rest of the stamp has slipped out of position. This instability is exacerbated by the multiple levels of image superimposition in the main part of the stamp – a homeless person sleeping on the ground, superimposed on the profile of a face, superimposed on the army choir, this pentagonal montage itself being juxtaposed with the more clearly delineated profile of the Salvation Army officer. The way in which the montage on the right is made to appear to emanate, like speech, from the mouth of the officer on the left, is a visual means of 'articulating' the proposed message of the Salvation Army. The instability of the overall design is further enhanced by the diagonal configuration of the textual elements which 'dance' across the visual image, the definitive message ('Nederland') being distinguished only by its slightly larger size from the commemorative message, '1887 1987 Leger des Heils' with the '1887' motif itself being aligned on an axis quite different from the rest of the text to which it is attached. While making the image and message more difficult to decipher, the aim here seems to have been to make the reading process a more rewarding one, both in relation to the message conveyed and to its graphic form.[18]

62

63

Auke de Vries effectively exploits the potential of image 'slippage' in his design of 1982 commemorating the centenary of the Royal Dutch Skating Association in which the skater in the bottom right hand corner seems indeed to be skating out of the image frame, the feet and lower legs having already disappeared from view (fig 62). The rest of the upper part of the stamp is left more or less blank, suggesting the white openness of the ice-rink or frozen pond, the definitive message stacked in the top right-hand corner (45 CENT NEDERLAND) being

64

65

67

68

69

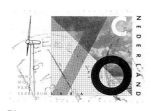

70

71

balanced by the national flag in the bottom left. In a set of five *Children's Stamps* of 1985 (one of which is illustrated in fig 63), Rob Schröder, Lies Ros and Frank Beekers, use the triangular format as a framework within which to explore the road safety signs which themselves adopt a triangular format, in accordance with established international convention. These designers resisted the temptation of making the perforation follow the triangular configuration of the image, each of the latter in fact being placed within a white rectangle, possibly to facilitate the production of the *se tenant* block of six stamps in the form of which this set could also be purchased.

Sometimes of course, as was the case with a number of sets issued in France to commemorate the Bicentenary of the French Revolution (see Chapter Two), sets of stamps are conceived precisely to operate within the expanded framework provided by the block. The possibilities offered here are exploited cleverly in the *Olympic Games* commemorative issue of 1992 (fig 64), designed by the German artist Erik Spiekermann, in which diagrammatic outlines of the pitches or equipment of five sports (volleyball, athletics, rowing, skating and hockey) are framed in grey rectangles, divided somewhat unexpectedly by perforation into only four stamps. The arbitrariness of the perforated divisions, which cut across the internal image divisions, creates a tension between format and image that is suggestive in some ways of the tension between the pitches within whose confines the sports are theoretically performed, and the occasionally wayward performance of the players who sometimes overstep the bounds. A sense of unity to the overall design is in any case assured by the rowing boat which, manned by four rowers, stretches along the bottom of the block.

THE MEDIUM IS THE MESSAGE

As has been the case with many British commemorative designs from the 1970s onwards, Dutch stamps in the same period have consistently drawn their viewers' attention to the graphic medium employed in creating the image, whether it be photographic, typographic, or a combination of various techniques. Sometimes the way the stamp image progresses up to and beyond the divisions marked by perforation reminds the viewer that stamps are printed in sheets and are thus only fragments of a larger image. This technique is exploited most effectively when the image is a simple and easily recognisable one, such as the tulip field (fig 65) designed by Karel Kruysen in 1973, the national flag (fig 66) whose 400th anniversary was commemorated in a design by Jelle van der Toorn Vrijthof in 1972, or the stamp designed by Otto Treumann in 1970 to commemorate the 25th anniversary of the liberation of the Netherlands (fig 67). At other times, design features within the image frame indicate the medium used.

In Karel Martens' *European Parliament* commemorative of 1984 (fig 68), the dot matrix grey of newspaper photo reproduction is deliberately emphasised in the photo reproducing a view of the Parliament interior, the austerity of the grey being offset by the primary colours used in the rest of the design. In one of Cas Oorthuys's two designs (fig 69, plate XX, i) commemorating electric train transport in 1964, the colour photo of the passing locomotive produces a blur of black and yellow, reminding the viewer both of the speed of the train and the way an impression of it can be captured by photography. In Wim Crouwel's classic modern design of 1970, commemorating the Dutch pavilion at the Osaka Expo, a photographic negative, reproduced in shades of silver, is the basis of the design which is enhanced by the beautifully co-ordinated digital lower-case lettering and the discreet incorporation of the Dutch national colours of red, white, blue (fig 70). Meanwhile, Stefan Graatsma's 1986 design promoting wind power uses a series of visual motifs – the designer's graph-paper, the colour photograph of a windswept sky, the engineer's profile drawing of the windmill – together with lettering, varying in size from small to monumental, to create a startling synthesis of text and image in which the commemorative and definitive messages of the stamp fuse perfectly (fig 71).

As Van der Toorn Vrijthof and Treumann's flag-based stamps show, colour can play a decisive role in both clarifying and simplifying the philatelic message. The simplicity of the Dutch National flag's design – three horizontal bands of red, white and blue – lends itself particularly well to incorporation in both typographical or figurative designs, while the colour orange, associated with the Dutch Royal family, can operate both as an index and an icon. In Wim Crouwel's design of 1968, colour in the form of a narrow band of the red, white and blue and the printing in orange of both the definitive ('Nederland') and the commemorative ('Wilhelmus van Nassouwe') messages, is sufficient to transform a simple typographical design into a message loaded with national associations, as is appropriate in a stamp commemorating the Dutch national anthem (fig 72).

In the 1980 *Europa* issue, the coincidence in colour of the Dutch and British flags is exploited cleverly by Pieter Brattinga in his stamps commemorating the close wartime links between Britain and the Netherlands (figs 74 and 75). A similar suggestion is made more discreetly in one of the two designs by Walter Nikkels, discussed below, issued in 1980 to commemorate the liberation of the Netherlands in 1945 (fig 81). The boldness of Brattinga's design is further shown in his reproduction, in the 80c stamp (fig 75), both of a portrait of Sir Winston Churchill and of a fragment in English of one of Churchill's speeches, matched in the 60c stamp by a portrait of Queen Wilhelmina and a text in Dutch. The Dutch flag again appears as a backdrop, supplemented by a band of orange, in Guus Ros' 1984 design commemorating the 400th centenary of the birth of William of Orange (fig 73) while a similar combination of colours forms the backdrop to the stamp commemorating the accession of Queen Beatrix to the Dutch throne in 1980 (fig 18). The use of a wedge of orange symbolising Dutch royalty is even more striking in Ton van Bragt's elongated horizontal design issued in 1992 to mark Queen Beatrix's 25th wedding anniversary. The orange triangle, derived no doubt from El Lissitzky's famous poster of 1919 'Beat the Whites with the red wedge', adds a purely abstract element to what is otherwise a montage of figurative images – two scenes depicting the Queen and her German husband. The stamp's curious curved framing bands, with a double perforation on the left hand side, further reminds the viewer of the 'constructed' nature of the image the stamp proposes (fig 76).

PHOTOMONTAGE AND COMPUTER GRAPHICS

Photomontage was one of the key techniques employed by avant-garde Dutch designers in the 1920s and 1930s which enabled them to produce visual images that were not like a painting in style and which could be made effectively into a collage both with each other and with the textual components of the message. As we saw in the first part of this chapter, the work of Piet Zwart, Gerard Kiljan and Paul Schuitema showed how such techniques could also be exploited to great effect in philatelic design. It is probably true to say that photomontage has, more than any other feature, contributed to the distinctive character of contemporary Dutch stamp design, particularly from the 1970s. What makes contemporary developments distinctive is the multiplicity of icons incorporated – three or four different elements often being incorporated in the standard commemorative format. A paradoxical result of this has been a certain iconoclasm, that is the

72

73

74

75

76

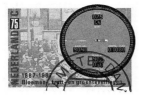

77

78

79

80

81

82

83

84

85

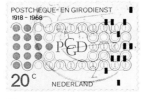

86

undermining of the monolithic icon's prestige as it becomes reduced to just one element in a syntax of images. This results in a certain initial illegibility of the image, a ploy intended perhaps to lead the viewer to interpret the image more critically; to read it as both a message and a semiotic construct.

In Victor Levie's design of 1987 (fig 77), the montage of a circular auction clock in colour against a monochrome photo of an auction of market garden produce expresses the idea of the passage of time implicit in the anniversary.[19] A similar ploy is adopted in Yoke Ziegelaar's 1992 stamp celebrating twelve and a half years of Queen Beatrix's reign, in which the monochrome image of 1980 is juxtaposed with the colourful shot of 1992, the textual message of the stamp following the slanting verticals marking the image division (fig 80).

In RDE Oxenaar's 1992 stamp celebrating the 150th anniversary of the Delft Technical University (fig 78), three different images of advanced technology are overlaid with definitive and commemorative messages, the digitalised '0' of the face value (60c) standing out by its scale as well as its typographic style. Jan van Toorn's 1991 stamp commemorating the 50th anniversary of the protest strike against discrimination against the Jews during the German occupation (fig 79), superimposes three elements, one photographic, one graphic, one textual. The way the typography of the textual message – Februaristaking – overlaps the montage of the central photographic image recalls Zwart's *Delft Cathedral Restoration* set of sixty years before (see fig 21). Meanwhile, the considerable propaganda potential of montage techniques is illustrated by Walter Nikkels's stamp of 1980 (fig 81) commemorating the 35th anniversary of the liberation of the Netherlands in 1945. This stamp is self-referential to the extent that, in using a war-time photo of a Lancaster bomber dropping propaganda leaflets and juxtaposing it with the colours of the Dutch flag, it in turn presents itself as a sophisticated propaganda image.

The advent of computer graphics in the 1970s once again presented a challenge to Dutch graphic designers, especially those who adhered to the design principles established in the 1920s and 1930s by the avant-garde movements. For these designers, it had been an article of faith to make the design image as contemporary as possible and to exploit, as far as was practicable, the technological advances of the age. The freedom, flexibility and sophistication of the image-making techniques made available by the computer was soon realised by Dutch stamp designers, though on the whole a relatively restricted number of commemorative designs have been produced which actually flaunt the computer origin of their designs. One of the first to do so was the 1970 set of Summer Stamps designed by RDE Oxenaar, who was also responsible for the design of Dutch banknotes (fig 83, plate XIX). This set, based on linear structures, was successful both in producing beautiful two-dimensional patterns but also, in some of its designs, in suggesting three-dimensional space.

The next landmark in computer-based graphic design was the definitive set of numeral stamps designed in 1976 by the artist who is perhaps the greatest modern classic Dutch designer, Wim Crouwel (fig 44). A comparison of Crouwel's design and that of Jan van Krimpen of thirty years earlier (fig 1) shows the striking degree of continuity within difference characteristics of Dutch stamp design history. The digitalisation of the graphic image is most clearly illustrated in René van Raalte and Gert Dumbar's *Postcode* design of 1978 (fig 82) in which the computer origins of the design are evidenced not only in the digitalisation of the lettering but also in the way an otherwise identical design is reproduced with the colours reversed – white on red in the 40c, red on white in the 45c. The use of digitalisation for the reproduction of a figurative image is shown in Peter Struycken's design for the higher value definitives issued in 1981 by the Dutch Post Office after the accession to the throne of Queen Beatrix in 1980 (figs 84-85). The image of the royal head is computer-based and appears either in grey-black on a subdued coloured background or in pale colour on a white background.

Among the reasons computer graphics may not have been more widely used in commemorative stamp design are the restricted scale of the stamp format and the need for a strong iconic image that is widely associated with the object, person or event commemorated. This suggests the need of an image that will be recognised by the viewer/purchaser of the stamp with the minimum of additional information. Although, as we have seen, Dutch designers experimented widely and successfully with purely typographic stamps, they have, like British stamp designers, recognised the potential of selecting an icon (purely textual, if necessary) associated with the object of commemoration and using it as the principal stamp image. Thus in 1968, Piet Zwart, in the last of his stamp designs to be issued, needed to do no more than reproduce a giro-cheque to commemorate the 50th anniversary of the Netherlands Postal Cheque and Clearing Service (fig 86). Jelijn van Der Wouw adopted a similar ploy in his 1976 stamp marking the 250th anniversary of the Dutch National Lottery Association (fig 87). The message that there are thirty-four different types of butterfly in the Netherlands is effectively made by Irma Boom in the almost life-size presentation of one the most common varieties – the Cabbage White – on her stamp issued in 1993 (fig 88). Joost Swarte's award-winning *Children's Stamps* design of 1984 lifts the strip cartoon format from the comic-book and reproduces it in the stamp (fig 89). A similar approach, although with some discreet montage, was adopted in 1983 by Jaap Drupsteen to commemorate the European Communications Satellite (fig 90), while, in commemorating *De Stijl* in 1983, Wim Crouwel had only to select a Mondrian and hang it on an easel to produce a perfect stamp (fig 91, plate XX).

The names mentioned in the last few pages – Wim Crouwel, Otto Treumann, Juriaan Schrofer, Gerrit Noordzij, Gielijn Escher, Karel Martens, Anthon Beeke, Jooste Swarte, and others – number among those of leading contemporary Dutch graphic designers, artists who have established a national or international reputation in poster and book design. Part of the strength of the Dutch stamp lies in the continuation of the tradition established by Van Royen in the 1920s and 1930s, whereby the skills of the best contemporary graphic designers are used, encouraging them to experiment with a wide range of media and to adopt a varied approach to stamp design.[20] Although this policy has from time to time produced stamps that verge on the illegible, that undermine the conventions of philatelic design, that exasperate some stamp collectors, or that tend to look a little like posters reduced to a minuscule scale, overall, it has paid dividends. From a design point of view, Dutch stamps remain the most sophisticated in the world and continue to offer the viewer or collector not only deep insight into Dutch history and culture, but also into the scope of modern graphic art.

87

88

89   90   91

92

93

94

Notes

1 This point is confirmed admirably in Alston W Purvis' recent study *Dutch Graphic Design, 1918-1945*, Van Nostrand Reinhold, New York, 1992, although only a couple of pages is devoted to Dutch postage stamp design.

2 The hybrid character of the commemorative stamp is noted by Gerard Kiljan and Paul Schuitema in the context of their controversial stamp designs of the early 1930s, in *Les Timbres-poste des Pays-bas de 1929 à 1939*, Publications of the Dutch PTT, The Hague, 1939, pp13 and 19.

3 In the Netherlands, these formats were standardised in 1965; regular (definitive) issues below one guilder in value measure 20.8 × 25.3mm; higher value definitives and all commemoratives, 25 × 36mm. See Hein van Haaren, 'Message Carriers: Dutch Postage Stamps', *Delta*, Autumn 1972, pp33-48. Hein notes that this standardisation has not brought monotony to Dutch stamp design. Moreover, since the 1970s, other sizes have been used, including, from 1995, a larger, 'Gentleman'-like format (figs 92, 93, 94), designed by Jan Bons, Julius Vermeulen and Aico Beukers.

4 The story of Van Royen's influence on design developments in the Dutch PTT was told in an enthralling way at the exhibition *Design in the Public Service: the Dutch PTT 1920-1990*, organised by Gerard Forde for the Design Museum, London, 1st Nov, 1990- 6th Jan 1991.

5 *Design in the Public Service: the Dutch PTT*, Design Museum, London, 1990, pp12-13.

6 This tension is explored by the Dutch stamp designer, Christiaan de Moor, born in 1899 and aesthetic adviser to the PTT from 1951 until 1967, in his study *Child Welfare Stamps in the Netherlands*, Netherlands Postal and Telecommunications Services, The Hague, 1969, pp20-26.

7 For contemporary developments in Dutch poster design, see *The Modern Dutch Poster. The First Fifty Years 1890-1940* (ed Stephen S Prokopoff), MIT Press, Cam, Mass/London, 1987. Paul Schuitema comments on the way the commemorative stamp can work as a scaled-down poster in *Les Timbres-poste des Pays-bas de 1929 à 1939*, p19.

8 A detailed reading of the iconography of this design is given by PAH Hofman in *Les Timbres-poste des Pays-bas de 1929 à 1939*, p41.

9 For more detailed accounts of Zwart's work as a designer, see Herbert Spencer, 'Piet Zwart' in *The Liberated Page* (ed H Spencer), Lund Humphries, London, 1987, pp151-58; Kees Broos, 'From De Stijl to a New Typography' in *De Stijl: 1917-1931 Visions of Utopia* (ed Mildred Friedman), Phaidon, Oxford, 1982, pp147-63, and Alston W Purvis, *Dutch Graphic Design*, pp61-79.

10 *Les Timbres-poste des pays-bas de 1929 à 1939*, p17 (my translation).

11 For the full history of the Kinderzegels, see C de Moor's *Child Welfare Stamps in the Netherlands*.

12 Cited by Benno Wissing in 'Paul Schuitema', *The Liberated Page*, pp159-66.

13 De Stijl theory and practice differs in this from that of the Bauhaus, if Laszlo Moholy-Nagy may be taken as spokesman for the latter when he writes 'Typography . . . must be communication in its most intense form. The emphasis must be on absolute clarity . . . Legibility – communication must never be impaired by an *a priori* aesthetics', cited in Philip B Meggs, *A History of Graphic Design*, Van Nostrand Reinhold, New York, 1992, p291.

14 Escher, in commenting on this design ploy, states that he adopted it so that the stamp could be stuck on the envelope vertically or horizontally, without impairing its legibility, see *Le Timbre-poste aux Pays-bas de 1929 à 1939*, p59. Retrospectively, Escher's squadrons of aircraft over the Netherlands take on a more threatening air, given the aerial bombardment of cities like Rotterdam during the war. One of the two Dutch stamps issued in 1980 to commemorate the 35th anniversary of the country's liberation in 1945 shows an RAF Lancaster bomber dropping leaflets over Holland (fig 88).

15 See Wim Crouwel, 'Type Design for the Computer Age', *Journal of Typographical Research*, no 1, Winter 1970, pp51-59.

16 As noted by Van Haaren in 'Message Carrier', *Delta*, Autumn 1972, p33. This modern attitude contrasts with that of the pre-war period when designers such as Sem Hartz stressed the importance in stamp design of combating the risk of forgery, advocating the use of engraving and the choice of portraits as a central motif, following the conventions of banknote design. See *Les Timbres-poste des Pays-bas de 1929 à 1939*, p65.

17 Cited by Kees Broos in 'From de Stijl to a New Typography' in *De Stijl: 1917-1931 Visions of Utopia* (ed Mildred Friedman), Phaidon, Oxford, 1982, pp147-63.

18 The design work for this stamp is documented by Paul Hefting in *Nederlandse Postzegels 1987*, Staatsbedrijf der PTT en der Sou Vilgeverij, The Hague, 1988, pp13-18.

19 Victor Levie's design work is documented in Paul Hefting's *Nederlandse Postzegels 1987*, pp53-58.

20 Not always Dutch. The Netherlands, like Britain, sometimes also uses foreign graphic artists, as for example Helen Howard, who in 1987 designed the stamp commemorating the 75th anniversary of the Vereniging van Nederlandse Gemeenten (Society of Dutch Communities). Her work is documented by Paul Hefting in *Nederlandse Postzegels 1987*, pp69-76.

Dutch Posters illustrated in this chapter

TOURISM AND NATIONAL IDENTITY
The Swiss Stamp

To commemorate the 700th anniversary of the Swiss confederation in 1991, the Swiss Post Office issued two sets of stamps. The first, issued in 1990 and designed by Ruttmann Hass (fig 2), uses the construction of the Swiss Cross motif in seven stages as an allegory of the establishment over seven hundred years of the Swiss confederation. The second set, a *se tenant* block of four stamps designed by André Bovey (fig 1), proposes a more ambiguous image. Taken individually, the stamps offer no recognisable icon; all one sees is an abstract drawing with a white L-shape in one corner. On each of the stamps, in the four official languages of the country, is inscribed the formula 700 jahre/700 ans/700 anni/700 onns. It is only when the four stamps are brought together as a block that the four L-shapes come together to form the Swiss cross. This image/puzzle may express in an elegant and economical gesture the idea that Switzerland exists as a national entity only thanks to the unity and co-operation between the four cultures. Alternatively, the Swiss cross may be read here as a sign of absence, an absence reflecting the identity crisis felt by the Swiss at the very moment when they were celebrating the 700th anniversary of their country. This second idea is supported by Hans Christoph van Tavel when he concludes his chapter on Swiss coins, banknotes and stamps in *L'Iconographie nationale* by asserting that 'Switzerland today no longer constitutes a choice motif for stamps and banknotes because feelings of national identity are loaded with too many question marks'.[1]

In exploring the use of national icons in Swiss stamps over one hundred and forty years, this chapter tackles the questions posed by the relationship between cultural identity and investment in the image. In particular, it focuses on the variety of ways in which national icons are promoted, discarded, adapted and transformed. The Swiss stamp provides an exemplary context for an enquiry of this kind since it emerges from both a heterogeneous culture and from a design tradition that is one of the richest and most sophisticated of the twentieth century.

The distinction between the iconic and indexical functions of the postage stamp that I have dwelt upon in confronting the design traditions of the various European countries in relation to philatelic imagery, takes on a special significance in the context of the Swiss stamp. Being a country of four official languages, for the benefit of its stamps, Switzerland has had to invent a name for itself that uses neither German, French, Italian nor Romansch. Thus, from 1862, the Latin formula *Helvetia* has been the identifying symbol of the postage stamps of the Swiss confederation. The word *Helvetia* constitutes of course a symbolic sign (in the Peircean sense of the word), but its use on Swiss stamps was from the beginning coupled with an icon, in effect the figure of *Helvetia* herself, who had from 1854 appeared on Swiss stamps.

Six different version of *Helvetia* (figs 3-8) have appeared on Swiss definitive stamps between 1854 and 1933. The first, the 'Strubeli' or 'Tätschgring', dating from 1854 (fig 3), does not yet bear the imprint 'Helvetia', but the Swiss cross on her shield confirms the country she represents. J Reiss of Munich's design of 1862 inaugurates the combination of *Helvetia* as icon and symbol (fig 4), while in the

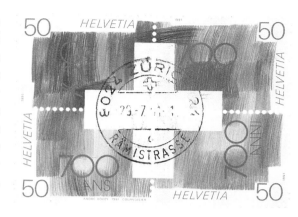

1

2

3   4   5

6   7   8

9   10

11   12   13

14 Charles L'Eplattenier 'Protect your Home Country.
Buy Defense Bonds', (Colour lithograph, 90x127cm),1936

stamp issued from 1882, a standing *Helvetia* is framed in an oval bordered by the twenty-two stars representing the Swiss cantons (fig 5). The three versions of *Helvetia* designed by Charles L'Eplattenier (1874-1936) at the beginning of this century, all show her against a distant view of Alpine peaks (figs 6-8). The first, dating from 1907 (fig 6) presents a half-length portrait of *Helvetia*, the Swiss cross emblazoned across her breast, with Alpine peaks at the level of her shoulders. The second (fig 7), dating from 1908, is a full-length portrait, with the distant Alpine horizon at the level of *Helvetia's* ankles. The third version, also of 1908 (fig 8), again a half-length portrait, gives greater prominence to the mountainous backdrop. The martial attributes of spear and shield, emblazoned with the Swiss cross, that decorated earlier versions of *Helvtia* are replaced in L'Eplattenier's stamps by a sword, whose aggressive potential is tempered by sprigs of olive or, in one case, oak.

Although the higher value versions of the 1908 design (fig 7) were retained until the early 1930s, the lower values were supplemented and then replaced by other icons. Was this because *Helvetia*, as a national figurehead, resembled too closely those of other European countries, such as *Britannia*, or even *Marianne*? If one compares the various *Helvetias* with *Britannia* as she appears on British colonial stamps such as that of 1860 for Barbados (fig 9) or with Marianne as she figures in the series of 1900 designed by Mouchon (fig 10), it is difficult at a glance to distinguish among them. This may be why her image was reinforced with other iconic attributes or ultimately abandoned in favour of more distinctive images.

After *Helvetia*, the most distinctive national figureheads to appear on Swiss stamps in the early part of this century were William Tell and his son. The latter first appeared on a low-value definitive designed by the artist Albert Welti (1862-1912) in 1907 (fig 11), reappearing in a slightly modified version by the same artist in 1908 (fig 12). Welti was an artist known for his sometimes apocalyptic vision such as in his painting of the *Nebelreiter* of 1896, and his stamp caused great controversy in Switzerland at the time of its issue, particularly on account of its juxtaposition of the cross-bow, instrument of aggression, and the innocent child. William Tell himself appears in a design by Richard Kissling (1848-1919) in 1914 (fig 13), based on his monument at Altdorf. This stamp was retained for the duration of the First World War and later reissued in different colours and values up until the 1930s. The more masculine and aggressive image Tell embodies may well have been a factor in its being issued during a time of conflict in Europe, helping to bolster the neutrality of the Swiss confederation that had been recognised since 1815. It was also used in the 1930s by L'Eplattenier as a motif in posters advertising defence bonds (fig 14).

Other national icons used on early Swiss definitive issues include the Swiss cross as a central motif in its own right and the stars of the twenty-two cantons of the confederation. The Swiss cross first appeared on Geneva regional stamps from 1849, for use on stamps issued by the federal administration in Bern from 1850. The cross appeared, as we have seen, on *Helvetia's* shield from the issue in 1854 and reappeared as a central motif in 1882 in a design by Professor Hasert (fig 15) which was in use until the end of the century. It next appeared in 1924 on a stamp designed by L Salzmann (fig 16), the artist who also designed a pretty, but not typically Swiss image for postage due stamps, also dating from 1924 (fig 17). The cross had appeared on earlier Swiss postage due stamps designed by Charles L'Eplattenier and issued from 1910 (fig 18). This design is interesting since, as with L'Eplattenier's *Helvetia* stamps, a view of Alpine Switzerland is included, this time further decorated with clumps of rhododendrons. The twenty-two stars of the cantons first appeared against a blue background on Switzerland's first official postage due stamps in 1878, designed by J Durussel. From 1883 until the end of the 1920s, a series of similar designs were issued in varying shades of green with carmine lettering (fig 19).

These heterogeneous elements were brought together and unified in 1914 in a set of three stamps that were to be a landmark in both Swiss and European stamp design. Created by the great Swiss/French graphic artist, Eugène Grasset (1841-1917), they were significant in three separate but related respects.[2] First, they were the first Swiss stamps to use the commemorative format in a landscape disposition, although in this case for high-value definitive stamps. Grasset had himself first introduced the commemorative format in 1900 using a vertical disposition, in this case to commemorate the 25th anniversary of the Universal Postal Union. It is significant that in his design (fig 20), the image of *Helvetia* is deemed in itself sufficient to represent the country without a need for the word HELVETIA to appear on the stamp. Second, Grasset's 1914 set launched the idea that the postage stamp, like the poster whose popularity was at this time burgeoning, could be used as an instrument of tourist propaganda by offering views of Alpine scenery (fig 21, plate XXII, i). Third, Grasset's set showed how the mountain view could work in the stamp image both to promote tourism and to propose an authentic national image of the country.

Although stamps focusing on famous mountain sites in Switzerland had been projected before, as in Eugène Cavali's design incorporating a view of the Matterhorn of 1901 (fig 22), and issued by other countries such as New Zealand (fig 23), Grasset's set was the first to choose mountain views – in this case the Mythen, the Rütli and the Jungfrau – that were attractive in themselves and that would strike deep chords in the hearts of the Swiss. Apart from the Matterhorn, which had received its definitive modern image in the posters (fig 24) of Emile Cardinaux (1877-1936) in the early years of the century and which had, in the popular European imagination, become virtually synonymous with Switzerland, it is significant that Grasset chose instead to concentrate on scenes that directly or indirectly linked the themes of landscape and nationhood. Thus, in the three franc stamp, he adapts his view of the Mythen from the great landscape perspective painted in1900 by Charles Giron for the National Assembly chamber in the Federal Building in Bern entitled *Die Wiege der Eidgenossenschaft (The Cradle of the Confederation)*, an adaptation that was reflected in further popular versions of this image.[3] Meanwhile, in the ten franc stamp, the view of the Jungfrau is accompanied, in a kind of visual pun, by a living *jung frau*, a young woman in Swiss costume, probably *Helvetia* herself since her left hand rests on the shield bearing the white cross, and the banner bearing the word *Helvetia* adjacent to her seems to refer both to her and to the country from which the stamp and the letter to which it would be attached comes. Here then we have an indexical sign (based on the symbolic sign *Helvetia*) working both within and without the stamp framework, in the first instance indicating an icon within, in the second indicating a referent outside the stamp. In this way the stamp offers an image rich in both visual and ideological overtones.

Additionally, in each of his designs, Grasset discreetly supplements his mountain views with further elements of national iconography. In the three franc stamp, we see the *fasces* of the confederation bound in olive branches. In the five franc, the view of the Rütli is supplemented with *Helvetia's* shield, complete with white cross. The ten franc stamp is enriched iconographically, not only by the visual puns noted above, but also by the stars (twenty-four instead of twenty-two!) that run down its borders, representing the Swiss cantons. This highly successful set was retained until the 1930s, although the three franc stamp was reissued in 1930

15   16   17

18   19

21a

21b

20

21c

23

22

24

25

26

27

28

29

redesigned by Emile Cardinaux (fig 25). Cardinaux's version has more in common with his own poster images (fig 24), clear, simplified, somewhat emphatic.[4] Its relative simplicity as a design anticipates the new orientation that Swiss definitive stamps will take in relation to landscape scenery in the following decade. Karl Bickel (1886-1982), as we shall see, will play a leading role in these new developments, and the direction his designs will take is already anticipated in his airmail stamps from the 1920s (figs 26-27).[5]

The shift from a definitive allegorical to a commemorative pictorial mode of national representation on stamps in the 1930s may be related to a number of factors. Travel by car and aeroplane as well as by train had made Switzerland accessible to an increasing number of visitors for whom the country had become synonymous with summer and winter holidays. The commercial value of tourism continued to increase and the country saw the value of promoting it through its stamps with attractive landscape images rather than with the more traditional national icons, often somewhat aggressive in tone with their spears, swords or cross-bows. The reputation of Swiss graphic design was continuing to grow. In terms of philatelic imagery, the Swiss, unlike the Dutch, never adopted the sophisticated photomontage techniques that artists such as Herbert Matter (1907-84) were regularly using in their tourist and air travel posters (see fig 39) – Hans Thöni's view of William Tell's Chapel, issued in 1938 (fig 28), was one of the first Swiss photo-based issues. However, stamp designers nevertheless increasingly sought the clarity, simplicity and typographic elegance so much in evidence in contemporary poster design and the use of artists such as Emile Cardinaux and Karl Bickel reflects this.

In 1932, the Department of Posts and Railways launched a competition for a set of stamps promoting Swiss scenery. Out of a thousand entries, the designs of the Bernese artist Eugen Jordi (1894-1983) were selected and issued in 1934 as a set of views of the Staubbach Falls, Mount Pilatus (fig 32), the Château de Chillon, the Rhône Glacier and Grimsel Pass, the St Gotthard Railway, the Viamala Gorge and the Rhine Falls near Schaffhausen (the set is illustrated in colour, plate XXI). The discreet inclusion of roads, bridges and railways lines in some of these designs hinted at the tourist transport as well as the scenic message of the stamps. Since these stamps were designed as low-value definitive issues, they keep to the smaller definitive format. Two years later Jordi's set was enlarged and refined by Karl Bickel whose designs, even sixty years later, remain more or less contemporary in their appearance (fig 33; colour plate XXI, ii). They were so successful that they were reissued in new colours in 1948. But Bickel's masterpiece in this genre dates from 1949 when he produced a set of stamps marking the centenary of the Swiss Post Office (fig 34, colour plate XXI, iii). This set of sixteen stamps clarifies and makes explicit the transport and technology themes implicit in some of the 1930s landscape designs, the slightly wider, postcard-shape format permitting a view that is both expansive and focused, the overall effect enhanced by the elegant simplicity and proportions of the lettering.[6]

The peculiarly Swiss link between mountain scenery, tourism and technology is worth pursuing since it tells us much about Swiss stamp design and about the expression of national identity through art, especially since the 1930s. An illuminating example is provided by the work of Hans Erni, who was born in 1909 and became one of the best known Swiss artists of this century and who, as we shall see below, made a significant contribution to Swiss postage stamp design. In 1939, Erni was commissioned to paint a giant mural entitled *Switzerland, the World's Vacation Land* for the rear wall of a model hotel designed by the architect Otto Dräyer for the Swiss National Exhibition in Zürich (an event commemorated in stamps designed by Karl Bickel, see fig 68 below). Apart from its size, the striking feature of this work was the extraordinary montage-like technique Erni used in juxtaposing against a vast backdrop of Alpine scenery, aspects of Swiss history, culture and technology (figs 35-36). As Stanislaus von Moos shows in his detailed study of Erni's mural, the juxtaposition of an Alpine bus and a traditional procession or a Swissair DC3 with exotic plants, expresses both the content of the Swiss scene and how it is expressed: 'technology . . . is not only the subject of Erni's monumental picture, it is also its *raison d'être*: the notorious industriousness and cleanliness of the Swiss are not merely subject matter but are part of painterly habitus and form'.[7]

30

31   32

Erni's project of 1939 confirmed the perspectives opened out by Swiss poster design of the 1920s and 1930s; the hairpin bends, electric railways, buses and modern aircraft of Erni's mural clearly owing a debt to poster artists such as Niklaus Stoecklin, Eric de Coulon, Walter Matter and Walter Reber, as is shown by these artists' posters of 1925, 1928, 1935 and 1936 respectively (figs 37-40). It also illustrated vividly the flexibility the alpine landscape offered to stamp designers, whether in the definitive or commemorative format. The choice of mountain views was almost inexhaustible and lent itself to combination with the widest possible range of subjects. In Swiss stamps of the 1940s and 1950s, the transport theme was particularly developed, especially in light of the promotion of modern tourism (figs 41-44). Mountain scenery worked well as a backdrop as the stamps designed by B Reber in 1937, Hans Thöni in 1953 and O Rüegg in 1947 (figs 41-44) clearly show. Use of the foreground was equally effective, as demonstrated by the designs of Edi Hauri in 1972 and 1965 respectively (figs 31 and 49).

33   34

As well as definitive and commemorative stamps, mountain scenery also appeared regularly on those special sets issued on an annual basis by the national organisations *Pro patria* and *Pro juventute*, as can be seen in the stamps designed by F Gos and Eugen Jordi respectively (figs 29-30), and by Franz Fedier (fig 48). These series, as we shall see, also explored many other national themes. The Latinisms *Pro patria* and *Pro juventute* again reflect the common symbolic language that Switzerland, with its multi-lingual culture, uses on documents of national importance.

41

Though most effective in the wider, commemorative formats (figs 28-31, 49), the landscape theme could nevertheless be accommodated within both the earlier, smaller definitive frame (figs 32-33) and the larger definitive format adopted after 1949 (fig 34). In 1973, H Wetli adapted the vertical format of the larger definitive frame to landscape views (fig 45) while in 1982, using the same format, Eugen and Max Lenz incorporated this theme into a set of signs of the Zodiac (fig 46, plate XXIV, iii). In a recent definitive series, dating from 1986, K Oberli, incorporates discreet Alpine vistas into some of the designs of his *Post and Telecommunications* set (fig 47).

42

This incorporation of other motifs into the foreground of landscape designs reflects a certain unease felt by the Swiss since the 1970s about the appropriateness of the mountain view as a national icon. The point was made brilliantly by Martin Diethelm (born,1943) in 1974 with his design for the catalogue of the exhibition *Schweiz im Bild – Bild der Schweiz* (fig 51) in which the image of the Matterhorn is superimposed on the towering facade of a modern tower block. The tension between modern and traditional icons, explored in Swiss poster design from the 1930s, has never been confronted in the same way by the Swiss stamp (figs 49-50); the latter was designed by A Cserno and J-J Chevalley, the former by Edi Hauri. This may be because, unlike the Dutch, with whom they share the reputation of a sophisticated modern graphic tradition, the Swiss have a less assured sense of their national identity. It may be that for them, the difference between the

43

44

38

40

39

37

45

46

47

48

49

50

remote mountain villages in Romansch-speaking Engadin and the bustling German cosmopolitanism of Zurich, are too great to risk confronting within the confines of the postage stamp. It may be for this reason that Swiss stamps have concentrated on exploring the variety as much as the unity of their cultural heritage.

After landscape, the most frequent theme in Swiss postage stamps was that of historic monuments, with which one may also associate the popular and decorative arts. Each year since 1913, *Pro Juventute* issued a set of stamps commemorating national themes, including costumes, the cantons' coats of arms, and from 1929, landscapes (see fig 29). Most *Pro Juventute* stamps however, especially since the World War II, focused on famous national figures or Swiss flora and fauna such as those (figs 52-54) designed by Karl Bickel, Hans Fischer and Niklaus Stoecklin.[8] It was, however, the annual issues of the *Confederatio Helvetica* and *Pro Patria* which, after 1938, explored most thoroughly the themes of monuments, sites, architecture and the fine or decorative arts (figs 56-59, designed by Stoecklin, Bickel, E and M Lenz, and Anne Oertle). The first in this series showed William Tell's chapel (fig 28), and from 1939 until 1952, each issue carried a shield with the Swiss cross (fig 55, designed by O Ruegg). Thereafter, a switch to the smaller format (fig 48) launched by Bickel's *Landscape and Technology* series of 1949 (fig 34), coincided with the dropping of the Swiss cross and the use of the *Pro Patria* rather than the *Confederatio Helvetica* formula. A new format was introduced in 1962, was enlarged in 1969 and brought with it new themes, including ancient coins, stained glass, archaeological objects, Swiss castles, artisanal signs, rustic furniture and so on (figs 58-59). In addition, from 1960, the monument theme was taken up for the first time by Swiss definitive stamps, although the idea for such a series dates back to 1942 when a public competition was launched by the Swiss PTT.[9] It was won by Werner Weiskönig whose later designs associated with this project are illustrated in fig 62. When the monuments series finally appeared in 1960, it was designed by Hans Hartmann[10] and Weiskönig, including images of postal history (figs 60-61 and plate XXIII, i) for its four low value stamps. The second series, which was issued in 1964 and also designed by Weiskönig and Hartmann, was devoted entirely to monuments (fig 63 and Plate XXIII, ii) while the third series combined landscape and architecture in the lower values, as designed by Wetli (fig 45) and artisanal skills (Hartmann, fig 64). These series of the 1960s and 1970s, with their beautifully engraved images of picturesque objects, maintain the Germanic vision promoted in Swiss stamps as opposed to the French style which predominated before 1930

51

52

53

54

35, 36 Hans Erni, Switzerland, The World's Vacation Land, project for mural, Lucerne, 1939, 100 x 5m, detail

55

56

57

58

59

60

61

63

64

in the work of Grasset and L'Eplattenier. This collection of stamps represents a significant part of Hartmann and Weiskönig's important contribution to Swiss stamp design.

Another important theme in Swiss commemorative stamps is that of national figures. Since 1927, *Pro Juventute* had habitually included in its annual issues at least one stamp celebrating a famous Swiss man or woman, beginning with Pestalozzi, the noted Swiss educational reformer born in 1746, as engraved by Karl Bickel. This tradition was taken over by *Pro Patria* issues from 1962. After 1932, other commemorative stamps celebrating the national pantheon were regularly issued, this kind of stamp becoming the speciality of Karl Bickel.[11] His famous historical series of 1941 (fig 65), re-issued in 1958, includes four portraits, and the image of Pestalozzi was taken up again in 1946 (fig 66). Bickel's skill as an engraver and his ability to capture the essence of the Swiss scenery and personality enabled him to dominate Swiss philatelic design for decades, especially in the 1930s-1950s period. An idea of the range of his ability is given in the series of essays he produced between 1922 and 1930 for Swiss definitive air stamps, some of which are reproduced in fig 69; those designs retained by the Swiss Post Office are reproduced in colour on plate XXII, ii (see also figs 26 and 27).

In addition to his landscape and figure stamps, Bickel also produced some masterly allegorical designs, such as the set commemorating the First Act of the Federal Parliament in 1938 (fig 67) and two of the three stamps marking the National Exhibition in Zürich in 1939 (figs 68a-b). From the 1970s, Bickel also collaborated effectively with other Swiss artists such as Hans Erni, as in the 1972 portrait series and the *Europa* set of 1986 (plate XXV, vii). Erni – painter, print-maker, graphic artist, designer – has in effect, over the last two decades, taken over Bickel's role as the leading Swiss philatelic portrait artist. His designs commemorating artists and writers of 1979 and 1990, engraved by P Schopfer, are particularly successful.

Erni was born in Lucerne in 1909 and studied at the Lucerne School of Arts and Crafts from 1927 to 1928, at the Académie Julian in Paris from 1928 to 1929 and at the Berlin School of Applied Arts from 1929 to 1930.[12] He had his first one-man show in Basle in 1935. He was much influenced by cubist art and by linear abstraction. Although he did not start designing stamps until the 1940s, his mature work as a stamp artist draws on many of the styles and techniques he perfected throughout his earlier artistic career. Thus the linear/organic abstract configurations of the 1930s (fig 70, *Emanzipation*, 1938, 36x34cm, Collection

65   65

67

66

ways of combining the presidential profile with national icons. Elements of the country's national flag, consisting of three horizontal bands of red, yellow and green, with a black star in the centre, thus often become combined in various ingenious ways with portrait photographs of President Nkrumah's face, as in figs 54-55 which mark Founders Day in 1960 and 1962. Even more ingenious is his 1959 Ghana design in which the head and shoulders of President Nkrumah are silhouetted against the statue of Abraham Lincoln (fig 57). This image, adapted from a photograph reproduced in *Life* magazine in 1958, is given the special Goaman touch in the way the name 'Ghana' is imposed on the torso of the African president, thus communicating, in purely pictorial terms, the stamp's implicit message that the great American democratic tradition of Lincoln is carried forward in Africa by an African president.[13]

A similar device is exploited in Michael Goaman's 1965 Malawi set commemorating the Fiftieth Anniversary of the Uprising in 1915 (fig 56). Here, the hero of the event, John Chilembwe, is identified by the imposition of his name across that part of the design in which his body figures while, overall, the text announcing the anniversary unfolds in the top right of the text exactly as the event it illustrates unfolds in the bottom right. A similar symmetry is established on the left hand side of the stamp where the heavy capitals of the country's name MALAWI are balanced by the solid-looking church building that forms the backdrop to the scene. In such stamps as these, Michael Goaman succeeds in producing images of poster-like vividness and appeal while at the same time reducing them to postage-stamp proportions, without any loss of legibility or visual impact.

The role of typography in assuring legibility and visual impact is also fundamental in postage stamp design. This is reflected in the Goamans' choice of lettering, their integration of it into the overall design, and in the way the typography strengthens and enhances pictorial elements. First their lettering. As comfortable using recess as using photographic processes, with each set of stamps the Goamans strive to select a typeface that enhances the message of the issue. The well-spaced, modern 'typewriter' typefaces used for the 1963 British *Freedom from Hunger* (fig 59) and for the 1961 anti-malaria issues (fig 60) express a clear, business-like approach to the subjects represented. The use of lower-case letters for the name of the country in the Fiji definitives of 1960 onwards and the Falkland Island *flower* set of 1968 was daring for the 1960s but more than justified by its clarity and elegance (figs 46 and 49). The Fiji solution was particularly effective, creating an almost logo-like image from the country's name. A similar

59

60

55

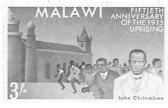
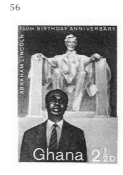
56
57

58

81

61

62

63

appropriateness and clarity is in evidence in Michael Goaman's choice of lettering for the engraved British Antarctic Territory stamps of 1963 (fig 61, plate XXXII). Here, he has given a sense of three-dimensional relief to the typeface used, designed in such a way as to provide a substantial framework for the simplified, even diagrammatic pictorial images he proposes of the Antarctic landscape. The typefaces used to accompany their flower designs – as in Sylvia Goaman's British Honduras 'Orchids of Belize' of 1969 (plate XXXVI, ii) and Maritime plants of British Indian Ocean Territory of 1975 (plate XXXVII, ii) are also exemplary – especially in their avoidance of the mistake, made by many lesser artists, of setting the lettering up in competition with the design of the flowers themselves. Using finely serifed Roman capitals, whose colours subtly complement those of the flora, Sylvia Goaman succeeds in creating images that are both scientifically correct and aesthetically satisfying.

A design feature that makes a Goaman stamp instantly recognisable is the use of text as a framing or compositional device. This procedure is shown in its most daring and simplified form in Michael Goaman's design for the 1963 Sierra Leone Red Cross Centenary commemorative which consists of no more than the Red Cross logo and burning lamp symbol framed by the message '1863 International Red Cross Centenary 1963 Sierra Leone'. (fig 62). The visual interest of this design is created largely by the lettering itself and by the way the engraved lines of the stamp pick up and echo the rhythms of the Red Cross logo and symbol; the 1/3 stamp is particularly effective, creating a wonderful sense of texture as well as of rhythm. A similar general approach is evident in nearly all of the Goamans' designs where the poster-like use of typography as a framing or vertical device often radically enhances the pictorial dynamics of the design. This is evident both when the textual message is long or short. In the St Vincent 4c commemorative of 1965 (fig 48), for example, the exotic figure on the left of the woman on the beach, who carries a branch of bananas on her head, is perfectly balanced on the right by the vertical bank of lettering topped by the face-value of the stamp and the Queen's head. A similar juxtaposition and balancing of text and image can be seen in the 1962 Fiji 3d. (fig 47). On the other hand, the long message communicated by the Falkland Islands Radio Communications set of 1963 is perfectly integrated into the stamp, in which – a further refinement – the country's name in very bold capitals is matched by the message in Morse code that divides the Queen's head from the transmitter image (fig 30).

Such design skills are enhanced by the Goamans when they contrive, as they often do, to place fragments of text in such a way that they indicate not only the general message of the stamp but also the specific object to which a word or phrase applies. Thus, as pointed out in 1960 by James Watson, an early commentator on the Goamans' designs, the territory name that falls at the foot of each of the higher value Kenya, Uganda and Tanganyika definitives of 1960 (plate XXX), indicates the location of the subject.[14] Likewise, Sylvia Goaman exploits the vertical format adopted for the British Indian Ocean Territory issue of 1975, to position the 'Indian Ocean' segment of the country's name exactly over the expanses of Indian Ocean that form the horizon of the stamps (plate XXXVII, ii). Similarly, Michael Goaman has his Antarctic skier in the 2d value of his British Antarctic Territory set skimming along the top of the letters 'Antarctic' (fig 61).

A final word must be said about the skill, vital in British colonial stamp design and demonstrated with exemplary flair and finesse in the work of the Goamans, of conferring visual coherence on the often heterogeneous images that constitute the 'set', whether short or long. Shorter sets pose less of a problem but the skill with which, in just four images, Michael Goaman tells the story of the settlement of St Helena after the Fire of London is vividly told in his set of 1967 commemorating that event(fig 63).

British colonial definitives traditionally consist of a dozen or so stamps running from low to high values that through a successive series of images present essential aspects of geography and culture of the issuing country or colony. Very often the latter, tiny islands in the Caribbean or the Indian Ocean, are obliged to include flora and fauna, townships and coastal views, native traditions and types, historical events or geological wonders in their inventory of images.[15] They also tend to include such bland essentials as airstrips and loading winches. The Goamans invariably succeed in the perilous art of making sense of such miscellanies by employing a double strategy: first, a rigorous selection of thematic motifs, with as far as possible, a concentration on one or two dominant subjects; second, the adoption of a format and colour range consistent enough to harmonise the elements embraced by the design without imposing too many constrictions.

In an age of multicolour, the Goamans without doubt showed the finest colour sense of any British stamp designers between 1950 and 1980. Their skills are manifested both in the colour design of individual stamps, in the way colour harmonies of sets are established, and in the way the colour of lettering is made to harmonise with that of image or background. It is noticeable that the Goaman's rarely use black lettering, preferring white or deeper shades for the background colour. Avoiding the bland white often used in British floral or natural history commemoratives, the Goamans are daring but inspired in their choice of deep or bright colours to set off the exotic species illustrated in many of their stamps. The 1963 Sierra Leone *flora* set is a striking example, with the plant Blue Plumbago set against a vivid purple background and the shocking pink flower Ra-Ponthi against deepest violet (plate XXXI). Sylvia Goaman's designs for *Orchids of Belize*, the Cayman Islands and Malawi (plate XXXVI), also Jamaica (fig 65) are similarly inspired, pairing bright colours with warm, deep background hues. The Goaman's response to indigenous costumes is also vivid, the native headresses of St Lucia, for example, being set against deep coffee-coloured or purple-grey backgrounds to good effect (plate XXXIV, ii).

The Goamans also succeed in exploiting the suggestive potential of colour itself in evoking background, climate or temperature. In the 1970 St Lucia definitives, different times of day and night are evoked through the changing colours of the skies which progress from mauve through turquoise then deep blue to deep violet, pale khaki and pink, the latter streaked with shades of plum (plate XXXIV,

64

65

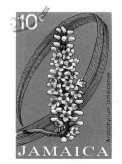

i). The cool blues, browns and greys of the 1972 *Tristan da Cunha* definitives (fig 64) invite us to contrast their South Atlantic chill with the sizzling combinations of turquoise and ochre, pink and emerald, scarlet and gold of the 1965 *St Vincent* definitives (plate XXXIII). Similarly, in the recess-printed series issued for British Antarctic Territory in 1963 (plate XXXII, i), the subdued blues and greens contrast with the hot purples, bronzes and maroons of the scorching central African climate evoked in the 1960 Kenya, Uganda and Tanganyika definitive set (plate XXX). In this way, the Goamans' designs succeed in evoking a specific tonality for each country illustrated or give the viewer a sense of the variety and range of the colours of some exotic climates. It is typical, that the Goamans consistently avoided 'new blue', a colour developed in the 1960s which disfigured with its photographic harshness many of the stamp designs of their contemporaries, especially those of Victor Whitely, who used the colour indiscriminately for the skies of the different countries, regardless of their geographical situation or climate.

The creation of harmony within a longish set implies an integral approach to its design as a set, not just in relation to the individual stamps. Such an integral approach involves reflection on design priorities and the establishment of a coherent framework of recurrent motifs. In his 1960 East Africa set (plate XXX), Michael Goaman considered not only the order of the names of the three constituent countries of Kenya, Uganda and Tanganyika, in relation to the landscape or wildlife views of each stamp, but also the corresponding position the animal icons of the countries – Kenya, lion; Uganda, crested crane; Tanganyika, giraffe – would need to take to work effectively as indexical signs. Furthermore, he had to design fifteen of the sixteen stamps of the set in groups of three, ensuring that each of the three country names was given due prominence in each cycle. The sixteenth stamp, the grandest yet simplest of all, summarised the motifs used in the preceding fifteen.

Sylvia Goaman had a different problem to solve in the commission she was given to design a set of definitives for Saint Helena in 1968 (plate XXXVIII) where the brief required a series of views of the most banal of subjects (a children's home, a dental unit, prefabricated bungalows, a heavy lifting crane, pest control, etc). She managed to create a harmonious and visually interesting set by devoting half the stamp's fairly generous format to illustration of the required themes in picture book style and pale colours, while devoting the other half to the evocation of five native plant types in the form of a garland around the Queen's head, triply repeated over the fifteen stamps. The set thus becomes a rhythmic evocation of Blue Gum Eucalyptus, Cabbage-tree, St Helena Redwood, Scrubweed and Tree-fern as well as of everyday scenes of life on the island. The final image – that of the John Dutton lifeboat setting out from Jamestown harbour, with its pale sea and ink-coloured mountains – is particularly evocative, offering a glimpse of the unexpected poetry of colonial stamps while also transporting us, if only for a moment, to the distant scene.

Of course, it is this poetic quality that constitutes an essential ingredient of the exotic and it was one that colonial stamp designers sought consciously to evoke. They were most successful in doing so if, as was the case with Edmund Dulac and the Goamans, they offered not the garish and undifferentiated images of the tourist brochure, but attempted to evoke the exotic using both real and imaginative elements. This involved using authentic thematic motifs – botanical species correctly illustrated, native artefacts or designs – which constituted genuine indexical signs of the country they represented, plus the construction around them of a coherent and aesthetically pleasing framework. Icons should always have a real link with the indexical function of the stamp which supports them; they should not, as in some recent colonial designs, merely offer images of Second World War aircraft, vintage cars, pop stars or Micky Mouse characters, labels which are not stamps in the true sense of the word but 'mere icons', stickers for the collections of juveniles. Philatelic art as practised by the Goamans implies the promotion of an alluring icon while at the same time preserving the stamp's indexical integrity.[16]

Notes

1 Edmund Dulac was born in Toulouse in 1882. He enrolled as a law student at the University of Toulouse but was more interested in art and completed three years at the Ecole des Beaux-Arts in 1903. That year he won a scholarship to the Académie Julien in Paris, but was not happy there so he moved to London where he soon established his reputation as a book illustrator, winning two gold medals at the Barcelona International Exhibition in 1911. He was naturalised as a British citizen in 1912. He became interested in postage stamp design in 1935, producing between 1937 and 1953 the most original and beautiful British and French stamps of the period. He died in 1953.

2 For further details, see Colin White, *Edmund Dulac*, Studio Vista, London, 1974, pp172-73.

3 See Stuart Rose, *Royal Mail Stamps. A Survey of British Stamp Design*, Phaidon, London, 1980, pp39-40.

4 Dulac expressed his views more fully in an article in *The Listener* of February, 1944 which is quoted fully in *Royal Mail Stamps*, p25.

5 For further information on this interesting episode, see AG Rigo de Righi, 'The Proposed Anglo-French Stamp of 1940', *British Philatelic Bulletin*, VIII no 8 (1971), pp3-4; Tony Gammons, 'Entente cordiale: the Proposed Anglo-French Postage Stamp', *British Philatelic Bulletin*, XXV no 4 (1987), pp80-83; and David Scott, 'Marianne et Britannia: la rencontre de deux icônes nationales. Un projet franco-britannique de timbre-poste de 1940', *L'image*, forthcoming 1995.

6 Michael Goaman, born in 1921, studied for a year at Reading University Art School and at the Central School of Arts in Holborn, London after naval service during the war. As well as stamps, he has designed lettering and typography, books, posters, illustrations and banknotes. Sylvia Priestley, born in London in 1924, a daughter of the writer JB Priestley, studied textile design at the Central School of Arts and at the Académie Julien in Paris. She married Michael Goaman in 1950 and their long and successful collaboration as stamp designers began soon after. During the 1950-80 period they produced stamps for over forty countries (mostly British or British Commonwealth) which are among the most beautiful and original of that period in the world. They also worked independently, Michael from around 1955 and Sylvia from 1965.

7 For further insight into the difficulties of designing British stamps in the 1950s and early 1960s, see Michael Goaman, 'Problems of Designing British Stamps', *Stamp Collecting*, 8 January 1965, pp665-66.

8 Soon after its acceptance, Michael Goaman's original design for the CEPT logo was in fact slightly modified by the inclusion of a dial and transmission motifs in the centre of the logo. This was required to express the 'telecommunication' dimension of CEPT activities, the original logo, with its horns, only expressing the postal part of the message (compare Chp 5, fig 34 and Chp 4, fig 79). Although Goaman's modified logo is retained as the CEPT logo, *Europa* stamps, which since 1993 have been issued within the framework of the Association of Public Postal Operators (PostEurop), have adopted a new logo designed by Stephan Bundi (for examples, see the recent Swiss stamps illustrated in plate XXVI, viii and xiii).

9 This stamp featured in *Gibbons Stamp Monthly*, October 1959, pp18-19.

10 See *Gibbons Stamp Monthly*, September and October 1960 and February 1961.

11 See *Gibbons Stamp Monthly*, May 1969, pp261-66.

12 See *Gibbons Stamp Monthly*, April 1969, pp225-30.

13 See *Gibbons Stamp Monthly*, XXXII, April 1959.

14 See *Gibbons Stamp Monthly*, XXXIV(November 1960) and January 1962. Interesting comments on Michael Goaman's success in creating unity within this set are also made by P Air in 'Some Modern Stamp Designs', *The Philatelic Journal*, October/December 1960, pp97-99. M Goaman's reply appeared in the April/June issue of the same journal in 1961.

15 The conventions of representation manifested by British Colonial stamps are delightfully parodied by Donald Evans in the stamps he designed for imaginary countries. See Willy Eisenhart, *The World of Donald Evans*, Harlin Quist, New York, 1980; reprinted, New York, Abbeville Press, 1994.

16 For a fuller discussion of the semiotic issues involved in stamp design, see David Scott, 'Semiotics and ideology in mixed messages: the postage stamp', *Word & Image* (forthcoming 1995).

FIRST EAST-WEST TRANSATLANTIC FLIGHT 1928

fig. 56

POST-COLONIAL IDENTITY
Stamps of the Irish Free State and Republic

With the emergence in 1922 of the Irish Free State, Ireland naturally wished to assert its new independence with its own stamps.[1] Until this time, British stamps had been the standard issues. The dream of a national stamp had, however, already been realised in America by the Fenians, who had produced designs inscribed 'Republic of Ireland' valued in US currency. A commemorative issue marking the centenary of the Fenian Rising in 1967, reproduced two of these designs (fig 3). From the beginning of 1908, Sinn Féin had also produced labels on letters promoting their cause, but later in the year, such labels were returned to their senders. One of the designs used, however, was later adopted on the new official definitives of 1923. The fact that the Fenian revolutionaries were fantasising at such an early stage about postage stamp design for their dreamed-of republic, is symptomatic of the profound role stamps play in the expression of national aspirations and identity, not simply in Ireland but elsewhere in the world.

1 2

3

4 5

6 7

In 1922, however, before a new Irish national set could be produced, the young Free State contented itself with overprints of the standard George V issues. The first of these appeared in February 1922 (fig 1) overprinted in Irish *Rialtas Sealadach nah Eireann 1922* (Provisional Government of Ireland, 1922). These were followed at the end of the year by a fresh overprint *Saorstát Eireann 1922* (The Irish Free State, 1922). The high values of this latter overprint series (fig 2 shows the 2/6 stamp) were to be used in Ireland for a further fifteen years until they were finally replaced in 1937 by an Irish design. The new Irish low-value definitives were produced, however, with remarkable swiftness and efficiency, as James A Mackay observes:

> The stamps were a rare example of Anglo-Irish co-operation coming so soon after the troubled times which led to the emergence of the Free State. The dies were engraved and the plates made at the Royal Mint, and the paper was made in Kent and gummed in London. The plates and paper were then sent to Ireland where the stamps were typographed at Dublin Castle under the supervision of a printer lent by the Board of the Inland Revenue (Stamping Branch), Somerset House. The stamps were then returned to London for perforation, since the Castle machine was not yet ready, and finally returned to Ireland for release.[2]

The first stamp to appear in December 1922 was the 2p green, designed by James Ingram (fig 4) showing the map of Ireland. It included the six counties which had elected to remain part of the United Kingdom although, of course, county boundaries were not marked. This stamp appeared on Irish letters for the next forty years and the fiftieth anniversary of its introduction was commemorated in 1972. Irish artists were responsible for the design of this and three other definitive designs which appeared the following year (figs 5-7). Following the brief issued by the Irish Post Office, these stamps were heavily symbolic in design, incorporating such motifs as the harp, map of Ireland, shamrock, the Celtic cross and the Celtic knot. The 3p and 10p values (fig 5) were designed by Lily Williams (1874-1940), a Dublin artist well known for her portraits at the Royal Hibernian

8

9

10

11

12

13

14

15

16

17

18

Academy (RHA), and were an adaptation of her designs for Sinn Féin covers, based on the twelfth-century cross in the National Museum, Dublin. The ¹/2 p, 5p and 1s (fig 6), designed by another Dublin artist, John O'Reilly, was an ellipse surrounded by Celtic ornament, within which there is a hand clasping a sword and the inscription *An Claidheamh Soluis* (The Sword of Light). This was the name of a journal edited by Padraic Pearse, one of the leaders of the 1916 Rising. The 2¹/2p, 4p and 9p stamps (fig 7), designed by Millicent Grace Girling, showed the Irish coat-of-arms comprising Leinster (Irish harp), Connaught (Eagle and Sword held by arm), Ulster (Red Hand) and Munster (three antique crowns). The three new Irish high value stamps (fig 9), designed by Richard J King and depicting St Patrick, appeared in 1937. Also designed by King were the two small commemorative issues used in 1944 to mark the tercentenary of the death of Micheál O Cléirigh (fig 8); from that date, they became definitives superseding the previous ¹/2p and 1s designs. They show O Cléirigh, one of the four historians of the Annals, embraced by the 'E' of Eire, and carry in Irish the inscription: 'For the Glory of God and the Honour of Ireland'. The myth of Ireland as a land of saints and scholars is thus already given full expression by Irish stamps within two decades of the emergence of the Free State.

The 'Irish' nature of the symbolism used in Irish stamps of this period is also reinforced by the use of colour. The national colour – green – appeared on the standard letter-rate value of 2p, later changing to orange, a change that was exploited to specific Nationalist purpose, as I shall show below. An early exception was the stamp commemorating the bicentenary of the Royal Dublin Society (RDS) in 1931, designed by G Atkinson (fig10). This stamp was blue instead of green, as 'a mark of deference to the society whose flag was blue'.[3] Green was also the colour of the lowest defintive value (¹/2p) and the cheapest of the larger definitives, the 1937 half crown representing St Patrick. The colour green continued to be a significant theme in Irish stamps, especially in conjunction with the use of orange and white, the two other colours that make up the Irish national flag.

The thirty-year period between 1929 and 1959 embraces two distinct and important phases in the development and presentation of Irish culture and identity through stamp design. The chief symptomatic elements at work here are the choice of language (Irish, English or Latin) and the choice of commemorative themes. Of the thirty-four commemorative issues in this period, twelve celebrated Irish political/nationalist events or anniversaries; nine, religious festivals or days; six, cultural topics, including two poets (James Mangan, fig 14, and Thomas Moore), the Gaelic League, the Gaelic Athletic Association (fig 12), the Catholic University (Cardinal Newman) and Ireland at home (*An Tóstal*); three, economic themes; two America-related topics (the US remains a central theme); one science (the centenary of William Rowan Hamilton's quaternions); and one other (the centenary of the death of Admiral William Brown, founder of Argentina's navy). Of these thirty-four stamps, sixteen used the Irish language (including fourteen of the first seventeen), ten were in English, the first of which was the William Rowan Hamilton commemorative of 1943 as science was still considered 'British', four were bilingual English/Irish, three in Latin (reflecting the strong influence of the Catholic Church), and one bilingual Latin-Irish.

Irish stamp design for the first twenty-five years of the Free State (1922-49) thus promoted a strongly nationalist and religious picture of the Irish cultural identity, with an emphasis on the Irish language. The declaration of the Republic in 1949 represents an important turning point. As far as stamps are concerned, it is marked in Irish stamps by a notable shift in thematic emphasis and the sudden emergence of a more *cultural* identity in terms of literary, historical, economic matters, as opposed to specifically religious or political images. This was also accompanied by a shift to a bilingual presentation of content. Indeed, by the 1950s, figures and events are most commonly presented in English. The linguistic, cultural and ideological diversification seems to reflect the new confidence of the Republic, and also a period of economic expansion after the austere and isolated war years.

The 1950s also marked an important transitional period in the field of Irish stamp design. The artist who had set the tone of Irish stamps from the 1930s was Richard King. As well as designing the definitives already mentioned (figs 8-9), and the Irish airmail set, *Vox hibernica* (figs 17-20), he also designed a notable proportion of the commemoratives of the period (figs 11-16). His stamps were mostly sombre in colour, often using muddy greens and browns, highly stylised in design, with extensive use of Celtic and Byzantine motifs, and used a wide range of typographical styles, often on the same stamp, as in the *Parnell/Davitt* issue of 1946 (fig 16) or the *Mangan* of 1949 (fig 14). As designs, they are, with the exception of the airmail stamps (figs 17-20) neither particularly legible nor beautiful and today they look dated. By comparison, George Atkinson's designs (figs 10, 21 and 22) and that of EL Lawrenson (fig 23) are simpler, clearer and more modern in their anticipation of the uncluttered style of the early 1960s designs. Recess printing by de la Rue of Dublin in the 1950s, as opposed to the typographical process of the previous decades, also helped promote a new clarity of image.

The appearance of the second definitive series from 1968, that was used until 1982, marks a new European presentation of Ireland's image through its stamps. The work of the German designer Heinrich Gerl uses Celtic motifs to great effect, half of which were drawn from English sources (figs 24-27). There is a certain paradox in Irish stamp design that reflects the wider problem of an Irish culture which strives to be both Irish and European; and yet the latter ambition involves a certain re-attachment to the British tradition from which Irish culture is trying to create a separate identity. The simplicity of Gerl's designs contrasts with the quaint decorativeness of the earlier definitive set. However, a subtle colour symbolism still prevails – about one third of the lower-value stamps appear in shades of green.

Irish commemorative stamps of the 1960s to early 1970s continue the process of European modernisation of Irish stamp design. The main motif of the annual *Europa* issues (1960-1973, with a break in 1961) was each year that they be designed by an artist from a different European country. In 1970 it was the Irishman Louis Le Brocquy (fig 28) who began to give a European look to Irish stamps, which were to attract the interest of European collectors. But this Europeanism was accompanied by a resurgence of the use of the Irish language in commemorative issues, as can be seen in another design by Le Brocquy, commemorating Irish Membership of the EC (fig 29).

The 1960s was also a period of revival of the nationalist spirit, prompted in some measure by the 50th anniversary of the Easter Rising in 1916 and of the deaths of a number of Irish patriots then or soon after. Of the sixty-odd commemoratives issued in the 1960-1973 period, eighteen were associated with nationalist anniversaries. The most famous set was that designed by Raymond Kyne, with a sunburst by Edward Delaney, issued in 1966 (figs 30-31) where once again, green is the predominant hue. The resurgence of nationalist feeling is just balanced by internationalist commemorations. However, the significant development in this period for the future evolution of Irish stamps was the emergence of an increasing number of literary, artistic and cultural issues, such as the Irish artist series begun in 1969 (fig 32). This series created a greater impact after 1973

19

20

22

21

23

24

25

26

27

28

29

30

30

31

31

32

33

35

34

36

when Irish commemorative stamps began to be upgraded to the British 'Gentleman' format. For stamps in this series of the 1970s and 1980s, see plate XXXIX.

This movement towards cultural interest in a wider sense is reflected in the third Irish definitive series, issued from 1982 to 1989. Based on line drawings by Michael Craig, the set continues the orientation towards the European formula. In terms of format, colour and theme, the definitive-size stamps, are directly comparable to West German definitives of the period showing castles or other buildings of architectural interest (compare figs 33 and 34), while the double-definitive format, with its engraved images of churches, castles and other notable Irish buildings, is similar to the French *Sites et monuments* tourist series that had been issued from the 1930s (figs 35-36). This set was not very popular in Ireland, perhaps because the colours were too muted, or because it did not promote a particularly 'Irish' image. This shortcoming, if indeed it is one, has been corrected in the current definitive series, also designed by Michael Craig, which shows artefacts from the National Museum in Dublin (plate XLI). This series is by far the most successful to date,

The adoption from 1973 by Irish stamps of the larger commemorative format designed by David Gentleman, used systematically in Great Britain from 1971, heralded an approach to both style and theme that has had a marked and continuing effect on Irish stamp design. The first use, in both Ireland and Britain, of this new format for stamps commemorating the work of visual artists, underlines its pictorial potential; the first Irish stamp of this sort reproduced a work by the Scottish-born artist William Scott (1913-89) – see plate XXXIX, xi. As a result of this, both the role of Irish artists in stamp design, and the presentation of painting as thematic documentation as well as in its own right, were to play an increasing part in Irish stamps. This development can be seen as a further stage in the move in Irish design towards a more European style of cultural presentation. This was prompted both by Ireland's entry, with Britain, into the Common market in 1973, and the devolution from 1974 of the design of the *Europa CEPT* stamps to individual member states (except for the 25th anniversary issue of 1984).

From 1974, then, the annual *Europa* stamps offered the opportunity to display the Irish dimension to the common themes elaborated in the series. Thus the 1976 Irish *Europa* issue (figs 37-38), designed by the artist Patrick Hickey, showed eighteenth-century Irish china while the 1977 set, designed by the Irish-based Dutch artist Adriaan van der Grijn, was one of the first stamps to open windows onto the Irish landscape (figs 39-40). Two other memorable stamps in the Irish *Europa* series were those designed by Peter Byrne to commemorate George Bernard Shaw and Oscar Wilde in 1980 (plate XL). The fact that both these images were by foreign artists – Alick Ritchie and Toulouse-Lautrec respectively – and decidedly caricatural in their rendering of Irish literary figures, reflects a new maturity of approach to Irish presentation of its cultural heritage. A similar sophistication is visible in some recent Irish *Europa* stamps, as in the 1987 set commemorating architecture designed by Michael Lund (plate XL, viii); see also this artist's stamp marking the bicentenary of the Royal Irish Academy (plate XL).

The task of designing commemoratives orientated towards scientific or technological subjects fell, especially in the later 1970s and early 1980s, to two contemporary Irish artists – Patrick Scott, who was born in 1921, and Robert Ballagh, born in 1943. The designs of the most famous contemporary Irish artist – Louis Le Brocquy – had already been used to promote an 'Irish' image in the international sphere – Ireland's *Europa* design, already mentioned (fig 28), the *World Health Day* issue of 1972, and the stamp marking Ireland's entry into the EC in 1973 (fig 29). Here, the so-called 'Celtic' motif of continuous patterning, where, in effect, pattern *is* the design, are consistently employed, as they are in Le Brocquy's graphic and fabric designs. The Celtic motif reappears in the 26p value of the 1983 *Europa* set, designed by Peter Wildbur, but based on Le Brocquy's drawing of neolithic patterns incised on the stone of Newgrange, while Le Brocquy's inimitable style as a graphic artist is exemplified in his 1984 design marking the Los Angeles Olympics (plate XXXIX, i) in which the style of his *Táin* prints of 1969 is adapted successfully to the representation of athletic activities. Scott and Ballagh, on the other hand, were selected to explore the themes – new to Ireland – of science, technology and communications in part because they appeared as two of the most modern in their style as artists. Scott was a producer of elegant, understated landscape or abstract works, as seen in the *World Ploughing Championships* set of 1973 (plate XXXIX, iii), Ballagh as a creator of pop images, often hyper-realist in style – such as in the *Irish Theatre* series of 1990 (plate XLII, x).

37

38

The commissioning of artists as important as Le Brocquy, Scott and, slightly later, Ballagh, underlines the importance Ireland attached from the late 1960s to promoting a more modern and sophisticated image of the country. This point is illustrated by a comparison of the stamp, designed by Peter Wildbur in 1981 (fig 44), marking the 250th anniversary of the Royal Dublin Society with that of 1931 marking the bicentenary (fig 10). The early stamp promotes the image of a small, basically agricultural community, locked in its own language – Irish – and a certain nostalgia for the past. The 1981 stamp, on the other hand, stresses the scientific and artistic, as well as agricultural sophistication of the country in a clear contemporary image (the globe/computer chip) which suggests that Ireland has taken its place confidently in the modern world. The language used is that of modern science and communications – English – and the use of the colours green and blue suggests not only Ireland's national colour (green) and that of the RDS (blue), but also those of earth and sky. This stamp thus manages to promote an image that is readable as 'Irish' and yet that is at the same time attuned to a modern, internationalist conception of the world.

39   40

Peter Wildbur's RDS design no doubt owes something to Patrick Scott's example as a philatelic designer. Scott's particular talent was to take abstract or extremely simplified figurative motifs as the basis for designs in which the forms and placing of the images (in particular a subtle colour symbolism) as much as their figurative content, played the leading role in communicating the stamps' messages – as in the 1979 *Energy Conservation* design (fig 43). This stamp, like the one created for the *World Ploughing Championships* set (plate XXXIX, iii), owes much to Scott's paintings (one appears on a stamp reproduced on plate XXXIX, xii) and his carpet or fabric designs in which meaning and visual interest are created either around a dominant central motif (often circular) or a pattern of carefully calibrated horizontal bands. Scott's use of these techniques to give subtle expression to political messages will be discussed below.

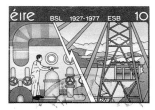

41

Robert Ballagh's stamp design commissions have fallen into three main areas, all of which to a greater or lesser extent reveal the way he is perceived as an artist.[4] First, his talent as a portrait painter has resulted in commissions to produce most of the recent Irish stamps commemorating historical or political figures, including Padraig Pearse (fig 61), Eamon de Valera (fig 45), Sean McDermott (fig 46) and Thomas Ashe (fig 47). Between 1986 and 1991, a special annual series, *Statesmen of Ireland*, was inaugurated, incorporating portraits by, or adapted by, Ballagh within a common form; the penultimate in this series, by Michael Collins, 1990, is shown in fig 48. This latter development was unfortunate in that it imposed a monochrome and confusingly look-alike framework on Ballagh's portrait adaptations which, hitherto, had introduced a more individual

42   43

44

45

46

47

48

49

50

51

52

53

approach to each design. In his earlier designs, Ballagh had succeeded, like Michael Goaman in his portraits of the black leaders of newly independent African states (see Chapter 5), in creating a backdrop in which some of the significance of the statesman represented was mirrored. Thus, in the Pearse commemorative (fig 61), to which I shall return, the rosy glow above the GPO building in O'Connell Street suggests both the fires of the 1916 Rising and the dawning light of Irish freedom, while in the 1982 design commemorating De Valera, Dev's broad shoulders form the horizon of a sky whose azure shines down propitiously on the morning of Irish nationhood (figs 45-47 and fig 61 are reproduced in colour on plate XLII).

Ballagh has also produced many stamps commemorating national and international organisations, festivals and cultural events. These include the *World Meteorological Association*, 1973 (fig 49), the *Universal Postal Union*, 1974 (fig 50), and the *First Telephone Transmission Centenary*, 1976 (fig 51). These designs, with their bold colour and simplified forms, adapted perfectly to the photogravure technique employed in most cases in their reproduction, typify Ballagh's early style as a stamp designer. Ballagh's skill in linking a human presence to a technical or cultural development is well illustrated in the 1976 design (fig 51) and in some later designs such as the *World Communications Year* issue of 1983 (fig 54), and the 1983 *Centenary of the Boys' Brigade* design (fig 55). Here, the profile of the boy, based on that of the artist's son, is balanced by the vertical disposition of the text in a manner similar to and as effective as that devised by Michael Goaman for the portrait of the Queen in a Fiji stamp of 1962 (see Chapter 5, fig 47).

The third area for which Ballagh has accepted many commissions is that of commemorating technical achievements. His designs include the *Electricity Supply Board*, 1977 (fig 41) based on a mural the artist painted for the ESB, *Natural Gas*, 1978 (fig 42), *First East-West Transatlantic Flight*, 1978 (fig 52), and *Dunsink Observatory*, 1985 (fig 53). Ballagh's sense of how to design the skies of his stamps is as clearly in evidence in some of his technical subjects as in his earlier portraits essays. Thus, the starry expanses occupy two thirds of the space above the dusky silhouette of the observatory in the stamp commemorating the bicentenary of Dunsink (fig 53) while in the 1978 *Transatlantic Flight* set (fig 52), the black outline of the aircraft *Bremen* descends vertiginously from the blue above a bank of cloud, the lettering in the upper part of the stamp continuing the sky area and thus enhancing the feeling of space. The artwork for this stamp, with cloud studies and aircraft silhouette, is illustrated in fig 56.

Ireland, though a small country on the margin of two major cultural nexuses – Britain and continental Europe – has mostly attempted to promote an authentic image of its cultural identity rather than resort to the vacuous neologisms or characterless glamour promoted by some small Southern European, Near Eastern or West African states. Its early tendency was, as I have shown, contractionist rather than expansionist, its early designs being small, sombrely coloured and complicatedly symbolic. With a greater feeling of national self-confidence has come a more expansionist phase, marked in particular from the 1970s by the adoption of the larger 'Gentleman' format. But even in some of its most recent designs, Ireland has continued to orchestrate the various sign systems at its disposal – linguistic, colour-related, iconographic – in an attempt to produce an image both acceptably modern and legible on an international level, yet at the same time, Irish. In the final part of this chapter I shall show, using specific examples relating to the use of colour, icon (in this case the Irish national flag) and historical tradition, how contemporary Irish stamp designs have achieved this.

In 1941, it was possible to use the small Irish stamp to make a nationalist or political gesture simply by overprinting an orange stamp depicting the map of Ireland (fig 57) with the following inscription in green: *1941 i gcuimhne aiséirghe 1916* (1941 In Memory of the Rising of 1916). The land of Orange thus becomes green – a symbolic re-enactment of the achievement of Irish independence set in motion by the 1916 Rising. The three colours thus presented (the third being white) constitute, of course, the Irish national flag. This juxtaposition of the Irish colours with the map of Ireland has also been used in more recent Irish commemorative stamps. In his design celebrating the birth centenary of Jeremiah O'Donovan Rossa, Colin Harrison frames his portrait of the famous Irish patriot and member of the Irish Republican Brotherhood, set against the map of Ireland, with narrow bands of green, white and orange (fig 58). The national colours thus function both as decoration and as symbol, constituting a visual argument which obviates the need for any explanatory text apart from the proper name.

A similar economy of visual imagery is managed by Patrick Scott in his 1972 commemorative design, the *Patriot Dead 1922-23* (fig 59). Here, there is no text at all except the name Eire set against a deep green background, the message again being conveyed by iconographic and colour symbolism: the white dove of Peace rises against an orange sunset against a green background. Conor Cruise O'Brien, Irish historian and from 1972 to 1977 Irish Minister of Posts and Telegraphs, introduces his classic introduction to modern Irish history – *States of Ireland* – with a symbolic reading of the significance of the Irish national flag which, he says, represents Peace between Green and Orange. This interpretation has also become a theme in Irish stamp design. It reappears in 1986, the year the United Nations designated International Year of Peace. In Anton Mazer's design (fig 60), the white dove of peace emerges from the white central section of the Irish flag, expressing once again the desire for a peaceful solution of the conflict in Northern Ireland.

The most memorable use of the Irish flag in Irish stamp design, however, is undoubtedly that of Robert Ballagh in his controversial design marking the birth centenary of Padraig Pearse, leader of the 1916 Rising, in 1979 (fig 61). Like the 1988 Irish stamp commemorating the 400th anniversary of the Spanish Armada, discussed in my introductory chapter, Ballagh's stamp is a masterpiece of ambiguity. For, as well as ostensibly achieving what it was commissioned to do – celebrate the centenary of one of Ireland's most famous patriots – it also parodies and undermines the whole genre of commemorative representation, whether in the great tradition of history painting or in the more humble genre of stamp design. On both levels, Ballagh's stamp is richly intertextual. In its choice of icon – the General Post Office in O'Connell Street, Dublin (the Irish Bastille and main scene of the Easter Rising), the revolutionary bayonet and the portrayal of the young Irishman – this design refers back to the 1941 Irish stamp, designed by Victor Brown (fig 62) commemorating the 25th anniversary of the Easter Rising. It merely substitutes Pearse's profile for the first words of his 1916 proclamation, Pearse's name appearing in Irish against a green background at the bottom of the frame. A crude nationalist reading of this image is however tempered by the knowledge that this stamp is also a quotation from the French artist Eugène Delacroix's famous painting of 1830: *Liberty Leading the People* (illustrated in Chapter 2, fig 11). What Ballagh has done is lift the full-bosomed icon of French revolutionary zeal – *Marianne* – and place her in his own design where, as *Hibernia,* she becomes the substitute for the 1941 issue's bayonet-carrying figure. Ballagh changes, of course, in the process, the colours of the French flag from red, white and blue to the Irish green, white and orange.

Thus, in his Pearse stamp, Ballagh has replaced the more literal and threatening

54

55

57

58

59

60

61

62

63

image of violence proposed by the 1941 Irish stamp with a more purely symbolic or allegorical figure. In this way, he offers a wider European perspective – both artistic and historical – to the correspondingly *localised* action of the 1916 Rising. France had its revolution in 1789, he reminds the viewer, Ireland had its in 1916. Both are part of a long European tradition of striving towards freedom and democracy and both have to be seen in their historical perspective. Neither are the pure beginnings that mythical events constitute, though pictorial representation has tended to make icons of them. The fact that Ballagh's stamp is based on a systematic application of the principle of substitution obviously has implications for the ideological message it conveys. This was, in fact, a major preoccupation of Ballagh's own work as an artist in the 1970s and the Pearse stamp is a clear outgrowth of the series of silk-screens he produced in the early 1970s, based on European masters' depiction of scenes of political violence. One of these included Delacroix's *Victory leading the People*, 1971 (fig 63).

The Pearse stamp, like the Armada stamp discussed above, shows how complex stamps can be from a semiotic perspective. Such stamps constitute the tip of the iceberg of the nexus of cultural, historical and political forces of the society to which they give expression. This is particularly true of a small, post-colonial country like Ireland which has traditionally been dominated by cultural or economic influences that have had the centre or origin outside its own frontiers. In attempting to assert a national viewpoint or identity without openly antagonising the forces from which the country has in part liberated itself or with which it wishes, on its own terms, to fall in, a post-colonial state like Ireland will tend to invent images which are multi-determined in their semiotic intent, offering images which provide the possibility of a degree of independent or national assertion and yet at the same time do so without taking too narrow or specific an ideological stance. In view of this problem, it is interesting to note that Irish stamps in particular (from the late 1960s to the early 1980s, at least) have had such frequent recourse to artists or to the artistic image. For what better alibi could politics invent for itself than the aesthetic? And what images are more open to the play of signifiers than the multiple and complex codes of artistic practice?

Notes

1   For a more detailed account of the semiotic structure of the Irish stamp, see David Scott, 'Posting Messages: the art and semiotics of the Irish Stamp' in *The GPA Irish Arts Review Yearbook*, 1990-91, pp188-96.

2   James A Mackay, *Eire: The Story of Eire and her Stamps* , Philatelic Publishers, London1969, p89.

3   James A Mackay, *The Story of Eire and her Stamps* , p194.

4   For a fuller account of Ballagh's work as a stamp designer, see David Scott, 'Robert Ballagh and Contemporary Irish Stamp Design' in *Irish Stamp News*, Summer 1991, pp20-25, also reproduced in *Robert Ballagh. The Complete Works* Arnotts Exhibition catalogue, Dublin, 1992, pp27-32.

LIST OF COLOUR PLATES

GREAT BRITAIN
All stamps shown on Plates I-X are reproduced by permission of the British Post Office

Plate I
i   1935 JAC Harrison: *George V Silver Jubilee*
ii   1965 David Gentleman & Rosalind Dease (photo Karsh): *Sir Winston Churchill*
iii 1974 C Clement & E Hughes: *Birth Centenary of Sir Winston Churchill*
iv   1985 Bassford and Paine: *British Film Year 1985* (photos by Bill Brandt, Cornell Lucas, Lord Snowden, Angus McBean, Howard Coster)
v   1992 Why Not Associates: *40th Anniversary of the Accession*

Plate II
i   1984 Ronald Maddox, Trickett & Webb: *Urban Renewal*
ii   1988 L Trickett: *Christmas*
iii 1988 Michael Dempsey: *Europa – Transport and Mail*
iv   1989 Daniel Fern: *Europa – Games and Toys*
v   1994 Delaney Design Consultants: *The Age of Steam*

Plate III
i   1976 Richard Gay: *500th Anniversary of British Printing*
ii   1982 Peter Hatch Partnership: *British Textiles*
iii 1991 Howard Brown: *Bicentenary of the Ordance Survey*
     This design deservedly won an Italian Philatelic prize in 1992
iv   1992 K Bassford: *Europa – International Events*

Plate IV
i   1979 Stuart Rose: *Horseracing paintings. Bicentenary of the Derby*
ii   1992 Carroll, Dempsey & Thirkell: *George Stubbs: Paintings of Dogs*
iii 1979 E Hughes: International Year of the Child
iv   1988 M Swatridge & S Dew: *Centenary of the Death of Edward Lear*
v   1993 Andrew Davidson: *Sherlock Holmes*

Plate V
i   1976 David Gentleman: *Social Reformers*
ii   1981 John Gibbs: *International Year of the Disabled*
iii 1982 David Gentleman: *Death Centenary of Charles Darwin*
iv   1986 Nicholas Cudworth: *13th Commonwealth Games; World Men's Hockey Cup*

Plate VI
i   1984 F Newell & J Sorrell: *50th Anniversary of the British Council*
ii   1986 Brian Sanders: *History of the Royal Air Force*
iii 1987 Michael Dempsey, engraving C Slaine: *150th Anniversary of Queen Victoria's Accession*
iv   1988 E Hughes: *Bicentenary of the Linnean Society*

v   1988 Garry Emery: *Bicentenary of Australia*

Plate VII
i   1984 Howard Waller: *Centenary of Greenwich Meridian*
ii   1982 Delaney & Ireland: *Information Technology*
iii 1972 David Gentleman: *Broadcasting Anniversaries – BBC*
iv   1987 Sarah Godwin: *300th Anniversary of Newton's 'Principia mathematica'*
v   1977 Jerzy Karo: *Royal Institute of Chemistry Centenary*

Plate VIII
i   1985 Wilson McLean: Europa: *European Music Year*
ii   1991 P Till: Michael Faraday: *Electricity*; Charles Babbage: *Computer*; John Harwood: Watson-Watt: *Radar;* Sir Frank Whittle*: the Jet Engine*
iii 1991 Jean-Michel Folon: *Europa – Europe in Space*
iv   1986 Ralph Steadman: *Haley's Comet*
v   1993 Christopher Hall, Lewis Fowler, Sarah Warren, Alice Newton-Mold (coordinated by Trickett & Webb): *Europa: Protection of the Environment*

Plate IX
i   1973 Rosalind Dease: *400th Anniversary of the Birth of Inigo Jones*
ii   1981 Fritz Wegner: Europa: *Folk Customs*
iii 1983 Liz Butler: *British Gardens*
iv   1991 P Leith: *150th Anniversary of Kew Gardens*

Plate X
i   1991 Bryan Kneale: *Dinosaurs*
ii   1992 John Gorham & K Bowen The Four Seasons: *Wintertime*
iii 1993 Pandora Sellars: *14th World Orchid Conference, Glasgow*
iv   1993 David Gentleman: *600th Anniversary of the Abbotsbury Swannery*

FRANCE
Stamps in Plates XI-XV are reproduced with the authorisation of the French Post Office/ Timbres-poste reproduits avec l'autorisation de la Poste

Plate XI
i   1924 Edmond Becker: *Olympic Games, Paris*
ii   1924 Edmond Becker: *International Exhibition of Modern Decorative Arts*
iii 1935 Albert Decaris: *Maiden Voyage of SS Normandie*
iv   1936 Engraved by Degorce: *Chamonix-Mont Blanc Skiing Week*
v   1936 Engraved by Galanis and Daragnès: *Paris International Exhibition*
vi   1937 Gabriel-Antoine Barlangue: *Mermoz Commemoration*
vii 1944 Paul-Pierre Lemagny: *Centenary of Paris-Orléans and Paris-Rouen Railways*

viii 1941   Gabriel-Antoine Barlangue: *Anti-Cancer Fund*
ix   1946   E Mazelin, H Cheffer, R Serres: *Monuments and sites*
      1947   Pierre Gandon: *Monuments and sites*
x   1953   Pierre Gandon: *National Industries and Literary Figures*
xi   1950   Paul-Pierre Lemagny: *Famous French Women: Mme de Sévigné*
xii 1963   Jules Piel: *Red Cross Centenary* (David d'Angers & Manet)

Plate XII

i   1993   Pierre Forget: *Post Office Workers around the world sailing*
ii   1986   Andreotto: *Typography* (Raymond Gid)
iii 1975   G Lacroix: *International Women's Year*
iv   1991   *Max Ernst Centenary*
v   1992   ITVF: *Niki de Saint-Phalle*
vi   1989   Art Series: *Yves Klein*
vii 1978   Winckler: *Tourist Series* (Saint Saturnin's Church)
viii 1989   Jacques Jubert: *Tourist Series* (La Brenne)
ix   1987   Pierre Forget: *Tourist Series* (Azay-le-Rideau)
x   1984   De Joux/Claude Jumelet: *Air Post*
xi   1988   Gouju/Coatantiec: *125th Anniversary of the Red Cross*
xii 1983   Andreotto: *50th Anniversary of Air France*

Plate XIII

i   1989   Pierre Forget: *Personnages célèbres de la Révolution française*
ii   1989   Marie-Noëlle Goffin: *Personnages célèbres de la Révolution française* (second series)
iii 1989   Jacques Gauthier: *Personnages célèbres de la Révolution française* (third series)
iv   1989   Jacques Jubert: *Personnages célèbres de la Révolution française* (fourth series)

Plate XIV

i   1989   M Durand-Megret/Claude Jumelet: *Liberté, Egalité, Fraternité*
ii   1989   Alain Rouhier/Jacky Larrivière & Claude Jumelet: *Déclaration des droits de l'homme*
iii 1989   Alain Rouhier/Jacky Larrivière & Claude Jumelet: *Déclaration des droits de l'homme* (second series)

Plate XV

i   1988   Roger Druet/Georges Betemps: *1788 Grenoble Journée des tuiles; 1788 Assemblée des trois ordres, Vizille*
ii   1989   Jean-Michel Folon: *Bicentenaire de la Révolution française*
iii 1989   Louis Briat: *Marianne definitive*
iv   1989   Odette Baillais (after J-L David): *Le Serment du Jeu de Paume*
v   1988   Essays for the projected *Marianne* definitive to mark the Bicentenary of the French Revolution

THE NETHERLANDS

All stamps in Plates XVI-XX are reproduced with the kind permission of the Dutch Post Office/ PTT Post Filatelie, Netherlands

Plate XVI

i   1913   KPC de Bazel: *Centenary of Independence*
ii   1923   WA van Konijnenburg/Jan van Krimpen (lettering): *25th Anniversary of Queen's accession*
iii 1923   M de Klerk, SH de Roos, NJ van der Vecht: *Numerals*
iv   1921   Chris Lebeau: *Air*
v   1924   Chris Lebeau: *Numerals definitives*

vi   1928   Chris Lebeau: *Air*
vii 1929   Jacob Jongert: *Air (Mercury)*
viii 1924   PAH Hofman: *Dutch Lifeboat Centenary*
ix   1933   PAH Hofman: *Peace Propaganda*
x   1931   Gerard Kiljan: *Child Welfare*
xi   1932   Paul Schuitema: *Tourist Propaganda*
xii 1931   Piet Zwart: *Air; Gouda Church Restoration Fund; Wilhelmina*
xiii 1933   Aart van Dobbenburg: *Air: Special Flights*
xiv 1938   Aart van Dobbenburg: *Air: Special Flights*
xv   1935   MC Escher: *Air Fund*
xvi 1949   MC Escher: *75th Anniversary of Universal Postal Union* (Netherlands and Netherlands Antilles version)

Plate XVII

i   1937   Pijke Koch/Jan van Krimpen (lettering): *Child Welfare* (Frans Hals: *Laughing Child*)
ii   1938   Pijke Koch/Jan van Krimpen (lettering): *40th Anniversary of Coronation*
iii 1936   Pijke Koch: *Tercentenary of Utrecht University*
iv   1943   Pijke Koch: *Old Germanic Symbols*
v   1946   Jan Van Krimpen: *Numerals definitives*
vi   1948   SL Hartz, WZ van Dijk, CA Mechelse; J van Krimpen (lettering): *Cultural and Social Relief Fund* (Summer Stamps)

Plate XVIII

i   1947   H Levigne, S L Hartz, K Brinks, Mrs E Reitsma-Valença; *Cultural and Social Relief Fund* (Summer Stamps)
ii   1947   Mrs Eva Besnyö/Wim Brusse (lettering): *Child Welfare Fund*
iii 1951   Cas Oorthuys: *Child Welfare Fund*
iv   1955   SL Hartz: *Child Welfare Fund* (Master portraits of children)
v   1956   Paul Wetselaar: *Child Welfare Fund* (Master portraits of children)

Plate XIX

i   1960   Paul Wetselaar: *Cultural and Social Relief Fund* (Summer Stamps)
ii   1962   Paul Wetselaar: *Social Relief* (Dutch New Guinea)
iii 1963   Cor van Weele: *Cultural, Health and Social Welfare Funds*
iv   1970   RDE Oxenaar: *Cultural, Health and Social Welfare Funds*
v   1969   Jurriaan Schrofer: *50th Anniversary of International Labour Organisation*

Plate XX

i   1964   Cas Oorthuys: *125th Anniversary of Netherlands Railways*
ii   1983   Wim Crouwel: *De Stijl*
iii   1989   Donald Janssen: *150th Anniversary of Netherlands Railways*
iv   1991   G Wernars: *Public Libraries*
v   1975   John Stegmeijer: *International Metrical Conventions*
vi   1990   Joke Ziegelaar & Hans Kentie: *Centenary of Work Inspection*
vii   1987   Cees de Jong: Europa: *Architecture*
viii   1979   Jan Kuiper: *300th Anniversary of Joost van den Vondel*
ix   1977   Anne Stienstra: *50th Anniversary Delft Hydraulic Engineering Lab*
x   1972   RJ Draijer: *The Delta Plan*
xi   1982   Donald Janssen: *Zebra Crossings and Road Markings*
xii   1989   Wigger Biersma: *150th Anniversary of Incorporation of Limburg*
xiii   1985   Jaap Drupsteen, Gielijn Escher: *Europa: Music*
xiv   1980   Walter Nikkels: *25th Anniversary of Liberation of Netherlands*
xv   1988   Frans van Mourik: *Tricentenary of William and Mary*
xvi   1994   Walter Nikkels: *50th Anniversary of Death of Piet Mondrian*

SWITZERLAND

All stamps in Plates XXI-XXVI are reproduced with the kind permission of the Swiss Post Office/ Schweizerische PTT

Plate XXI

i   1934   Eugen Jordi: *Landscapes*
ii   1936 & 1948, Karl Bickel: *Landscapes*
iii   1949   Karl Bickel: *Landscape and Technology*
iv   1956   E & M Lenz (5c), P Togni (others): *Pro Patria Swiss Women's Fund*

Plate XXII

i   1914   Eugène Grasset: *Landscape*
ii   1923   Karl Bickel: *Air*
iii   1931   Emile Cardinaux: *The Mythen*
iv   1931   Eugen Jordi: *Pro juventute*
v   1938   Hans Thöni: *National Fund (William Tell's Chapel)*
vi   1949   Werner Weiskönig: *Centenary of Federal Post*
vii   1953   Hans Thöni: *Mobile Post Office*

PLATE XXIII

i   1960   Werner Weiskönig & Hans Hartmann: *Architectural Monuments*
ii   1963   Werner Weiskönig & Hans Hartmann: *Architectural Monuments*

Plate XXIV

i   1977   SM Muri: *Regional and Folk Costume*
ii   1982   SM Muri: *Popular Customs*
iii   1982   E & M Lenz: *Landscapes with Signs of the Zodiac*

Plate XXV

i   1975   Hans Erni: *Bureau international du travail*
ii   1949   Hans Erni: *Air*
iii   1964   Hans Erni: *Pro aqua*
iv   1975   Hans Erni: *International Women's Year*
v   1981   Hans Erni: *50th Anniversary of Swissair*
vi   1969   Hans Erni: *Opening of Planetarium, Lucerne*
vii   1986   Hans Erni: *Europa*
viii   1979   Hans Erni: *Portraits*
ix   1965   Hans Erni: *Pro juventute*
x   1966   Hans Erni: *Pro juventute*

Plate XXVI

i   1993   *Swiss Artists*
ii   1982   Claude Kuhn: *100th Anniversary of Natural History Museum, Bern*
iii   1988   Hans Hartmann: *50th Anniversary of Pro Aero*
iv   1980   Adolf Flückiger: *Anniversary of PTT Stamp Printing Office*
v   1981   Adolf Flückiger: *Opening of Technorama, Winterthur Museum*
vi   1976   Hans Hartmann: *Europa: Handicrafts*
vii   1983   Hans Hartmann: *Europa: Crafts*
viii   1994   Pierre Baur: *Europa: technology*
ix   1993   H Billharz: *150th Anniversary of First Swiss Cantonal Stamp*
x   1992   Rolf Knie: *Circus*
xii   1993   H Schelbert: *Landscape; Priority mail*
xiii   1993   Mario Botta: *Europa: architecture*
xiv   1974   Max Bill: *Europa*

FRENCH AND BRITISH COLONIAL DESIGN: DULAC & GOAMAN

The stamps by Michael and Sylvia Goaman appearing in Plates XXX-XXXVIII commissioned by the Crown Agents are reproduced with the Crown Agents' kind permission

Plate XXVII

i   1945   Edmund Dulac: *French Guiana*
ii   1945   Edmund Dulac: *Guadeloupe*
iii   1945   Edmund Dulac: *Martinique*
iv   1943   Edmund Dulac: *Réunion*

Plate XXVIII

i   1943   Edmund Dulac: *Madagascar*
ii   1943   Edmund Dulac: *Madagascar: Air*
iii   1942   Edmund Dulac: *St Pierre et Miquelon*
iv   1942   Edmund Dulac: *Cameroon*

Plate XXIX

i   1944   Edmund Dulac: *Wallis and Futuna Islands*
ii   1942   Edmund Dulac: *French Settlements in India*
iii   1942   Edmund Dulac: *Oceanic Settlements*
iv   1942   Edmund Dulac: *French Equatorial Africa*
v   1945   Edmund Dulac: *French West Africa*

vi   1943   Edmund Dulac: *French Somali Coast (Djibouti)*
vii 1942   Edmund Dulac: *New Caledonia*
viii 1944 Edmund Dulac: *France*
ix   1944   Edmund Dulac: *St Pierre et Miquelon (Mutual Aid & Red Cross)*

Plate XXX
1960   Michael Goaman: *Kenya, Uganda, Tanganyika*

Plate XXXI
1963   Michael Goaman: *Sierra Leone*

Plate XXXII
i   1963   Michael Goaman: *British Antarctic Territory*
ii   1971   Michael Goaman: *British Antarctic Territory; 10th Anniversary of Antarctic Treaty*

Plate XXXIII
1965   Michael Goaman: *St Vincent*

Plate XXXIV
i   1970   Michael Goaman: *St Lucia*
ii   1973   Sylvia Goaman: *St Lucia: Local Head-dresses*

Plate XXXV
i   1965   Michael Goaman: Malawi: *50th Anniversary of the 1915 Uprising*
ii   1959   Michael Goaman: *Ghana: 150th Anniversary of Abraham Lincoln*
iii 1961   Michael Goaman: *Nigeria: Universal Postal Union Admission 1961*
iv   1964   Michael Goaman: *Kenya: Inauguration of Republic*
v   1964   Michael Goaman: *Malawi: Independence 1964*

Plate XXXVI
i   1968   Sylvia Goaman: *British Honduras: 20th Anniversary of Economic Commission for Latin America*
ii   1969   Sylvia Goaman: *British Honduras: Orchids of Belize*
iii 1971   Sylvia Goaman: *Cayman Islands: Orchids*
iv   1975   Sylvia Goaman: *Malawi: Orchids*

Plate XXXVII
i   1975   Michael & Sylvia Goaman: *Nauru: South Pacific Commission*
ii   1968   Sylvia Goaman: *British Indian Ocean Territory: Wildlife*
iii 1975   Sylvia Goaman: *Tristan da Cunha: Sea Plants*
iv   1972   Sylvia Goaman: *Gilbert & Ellice Islands: Coral*

Plate XXXVIII
1972   Sylvia Goaman: *St Helena*

IRELAND
The stamps in Plates XXXIX-XLII are reproduced with the kind permission of the Irish Post Office/An Post

Plate XXXIX
i   1984   Louis Le Brocquy: *Olympic Games: Ireland's gold medals*

ii   1979   Peter Wildbur: *Direct Elections to the European Parliament*
iii 1973   Patrick Scott: *World Ploughing Championships in County Wexford*
iv   1970   Louis le Brocquy: *Europa*
v   1969   Evie Hone: *Eton College Chapel Window*
vi   1977   Patrick Hickey: *Golden Jubilee of Agricultural Credit Corporation*
vii 1975   Oisin Kelly: *Contemporary Irish Art*
viii 1974 Norah McGuinness: *Contemporary Irish Art*
ix   1979   FE McWilliam: *Contemporary Irish Art*
x   1977   Louis Le Brocquy: *Contemporary Irish Art*
xi   1973   William Scott: *Contemporary Irish Art*
xii 1980   Patrick Scott: *Contemporary Irish Art*

Plate XL
i   1974   Peter Wildbur: *Europa: Sculpture*
ii   1974   Peter Wildbur: *Bicentenary of Death of Oliver Goldsmith*
iii 1982   Peter Wildbur: *Irish Literary and Musical Figures*
iv   1983   Colin Harrison: *Centenary of birth of Pádraig O Siochfhradha*
v   1980   Peter Wildbur: *Centenary of birth of Sean O'Casey*
vi   1981   Colin Harrison: *150th Anniversary of birth of Jeremiah O'Donovan Rossa*
vii 1980   Peter Byrne: *Europa: Famous People*
viii 1985 Michael Lund: *Bicentenary of Royal Irish Academy*
ix   1987   Michael Lund: *Europa: Irish Architecture*

Plate XLI
1990   Michael Craig: *Treasures of Ireland* (definitive series)

Plate XLII
i   1979   Robert Ballagh: *Birth Centenary of Patrick Pearse*
ii   1985   Robert Ballagh: *Bicentenary of Dunsink Observatory*
iii 1985   Robert Ballagh: *Bicentenary of First Irish Aeronautic Flight*
iv   1978   Robert Ballagh: *50th Anniversary of first E-W Trans-atlantic Flight*
v   1983   Robert Ballagh: *World Communications Year*
vi   1979   Robert Ballagh: *Centenary of Boys' Brigade*
vii 1982   Robert Ballagh: *Birth Centenary of Eamon de Valera*
viii 1983 Robert Ballagh: *Birth Centenary of Sean MacDermott*
ix   1985   Robert Ballagh: *Birth Centenary of Thomas Ashe*
x   1990   Robert Ballagh: *Irish Theatre*

PLATES

PLATE I

PLATE II

PLATE III

William Caxton 1476   8½^P

William Caxton 1476   10^P

William Caxton 1476   11^P

William Caxton 1476   13^P

PLATE IV

9ᴘ Saddling Mahmoud for The Derby 1936

10½ᴘ The Liverpool Great National Steeple Chase 1839

11ᴘ The First Spring Meeting, Newmarket 1793

13ᴘ Racing at Dorsett Ferry, Windsor 1684

KING CHARLES SPANIEL
GEORGE STUBBS

A POINTER
GEORGE STUBBS

TWO HOUNDS IN A LANDSCAPE
GEORGE STUBBS

A ROUGH DOG
GEORGE STUBBS

FINO AND TINY
GEORGE STUBBS

9ᴘ The Tale of Peter Rabbit
The Year of the Child

10½ᴘ The Wind in the Willows
The Year of the Child

11ᴘ Winnie-the-Pooh
The Year of the Child

13ᴘ Alice's Adventures in Wonderland
The Year of the Child

19ᴘ The Owl and the Pussy-cat went to sea
In a beautiful pea-green boat,
EDWARD LEAR • 1812-1888

27ᴘ Yours affectionately, Edward Lear
EDWARD LEAR • 1812-1888

32ᴘ C was a lovely Pussy Cat; its eyes were large,
And on its back it had some stripes,
And several on his tail.
EDWARD LEAR • 1812-1888

35ᴘ There was a Young Lady whose bonnet,
Came untied when the birds sate upon it;
EDWARD LEAR • 1812-1888

SHERLOCK HOLMES & DR. WATSON
"THE REIGATE SQUIRE"

SHERLOCK HOLMES & SIR HENRY
"THE HOUND OF THE BASKERVILLES"

SHERLOCK HOLMES & LESTRADE
"THE SIX NAPOLEONS"

SHERLOCK HOLMES & MYCROFT
"THE GREEK INTERPRETER"

SHERLOCK HOLMES & MORIARTY
"THE FINAL PROBLEM"

PLATE V

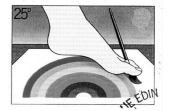

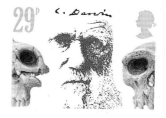

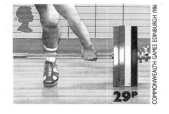

PLATE VI

The British Council
education for development

The British Council
promoting the arts

The British Council
technical training

The British Council
language & libraries

LORD DOWDING / HURRICANE

LORD TEDDER / TYPHOON

LORD TRENCHARD / DH 9A

SIR ARTHUR HARRIS / LANCASTER

LORD PORTAL / MOSQUITO

Bull-rout *Myoxocephalus scorpius*
THE LINNEAN SOCIETY 1788/1988

Yellow Waterlily *Nuphar lutea*
THE LINNEAN SOCIETY 1788/1988

Morel *Morchella esculenta*
THE LINNEAN SOCIETY 1788/1988

Bewick's Swan *Cygnus columbianus*
THE LINNEAN SOCIETY 1788/1988

AUSTRALIAN BICENTENARY 18p

AUSTRALIAN BICENTENARY 18p

AUSTRALIAN BICENTENARY 34p

AUSTRALIAN BICENTENARY 34p

PLATE VII

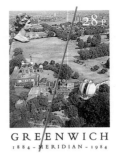
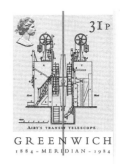

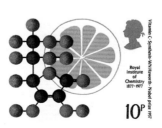
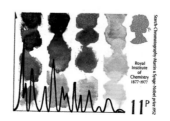

SEVENTEEN · PENCE

WATER · MUSIC
George Frideric Handel

TWENTY · TWO · PENCE

THE · PLANETS · SUITE
Gustav Holst

THIRTY · ONE · PENCE

THE · FIRST · CUCKOO
Frederick Delius

THIRTY · FOUR · PENCE

SEA · PICTURES
Edward Elgar

Faraday – Electricity

Babbage – Computer

Radar – Watson-Watt

Jet Engine – Whittle

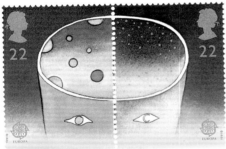

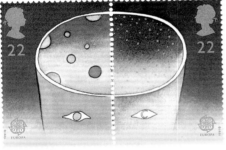

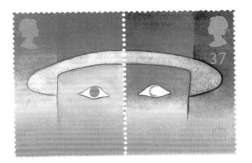

PLATE IX

20TH CENTURY GARDEN
SISSINGHURST

18TH CENTURY GARDEN
BLENHEIM

19TH CENTURY GARDEN
BIDDULPH GRANGE

17TH CENTURY GARDEN
PITMEDDEN

KEW GARDENS 1840-1990

KEW GARDENS 1840-1990

KEW GARDENS 1840-1990

KEW GARDENS 1840-1990

PLATE X

Iguanodon, Owen's Dinosauria 1841   *Stegosaurus,* Owen's Dinosauria 1841   *Tyrannosaurus,* Owen's Dinosauria 1841   *Protoceratops,* Owen's Dinosauria 1841   *Triceratops,* Owen's Dinosauria 1841

PLATE XI

PLATE XII

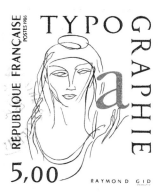

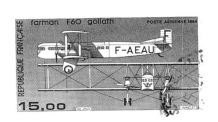

PLATE XIII

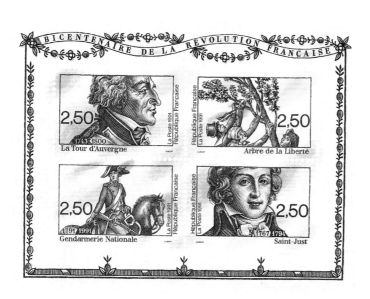

PLATE XIV

PLATE XV

Projets sélectionnés à « Philexfrance 89 »,
réalisés par F. Bernal, C. Bonnehon, C. Bridoux, C. Jumelet, J.-C. Mathias, C. de la Pattelère,
gravés par E. Lacaque, P. Béquet, J. Larrivière, C. Jumelet, G. Bétemps et C. Durrens.

PLATE XVI

PLATE XVII

PLATE XVIII

PLATE XIX

PLATE XX

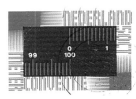

PLATE XXI

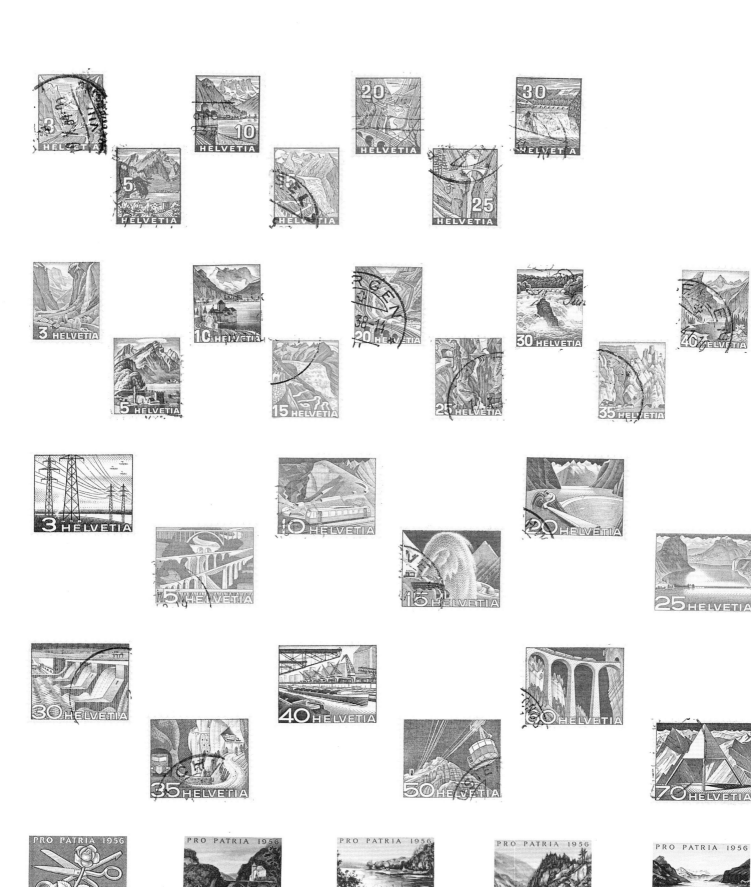

PLATE XXII

PLATE XXIII

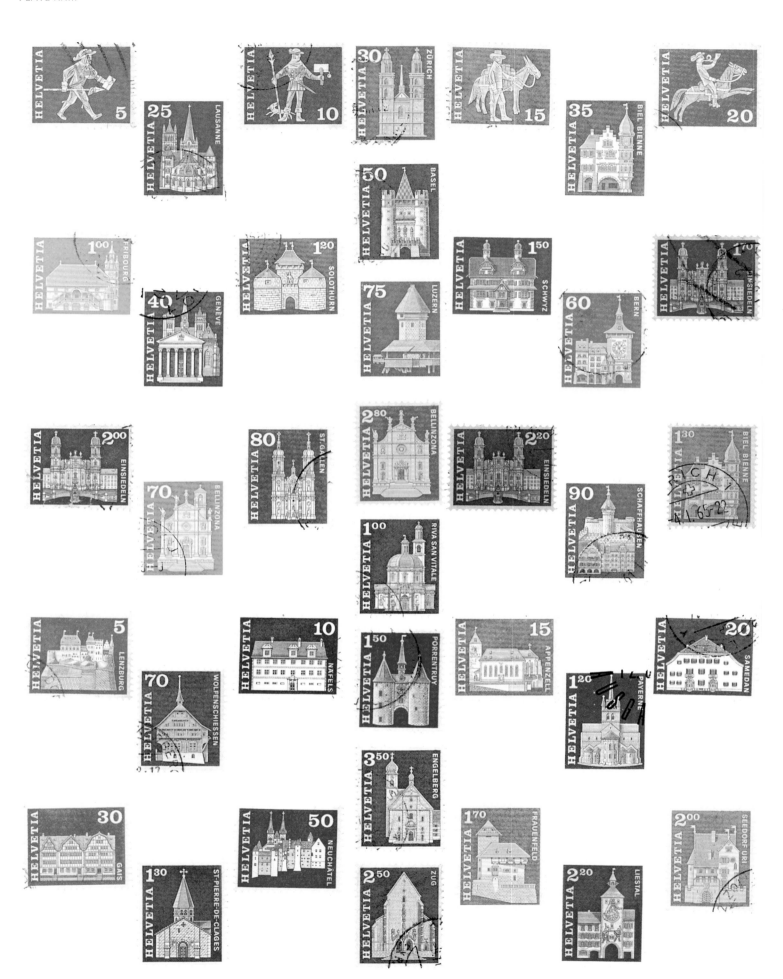

PLATE XXIV

PLATE XXV

PLATE XXVI

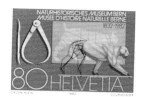

PLATE XXVII

PLATE XXVIII

PLATE XXIX

PLATE XXX

PLATE XXXI

PLATE XXXII

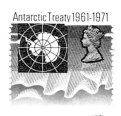

PLATE XXXIII

PLATE XXXIV

PLATE XXXV

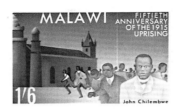

PLATE XXXVI

PLATE XXXVII

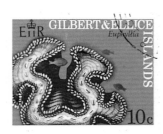

PLATE XXXVIII

ROAD CONSTRUCTION
½d St.Helena

ELECTRICITY DEVELOPMENT
1d St.Helena

DENTAL UNIT
1½d St.Helena

PEST CONTROL
2d St.Helena

FLATS IN JAMESTOWN
3d St.Helena

PASTURE AND LIVESTOCK IMPROVEMENT
4d St.Helena

SCHOOLS BROADCASTING
6d St.Helena

COUNTRY COTTAGES
8d St.Helena

NEW SCHOOL BUILDINGS
10d St.Helena

REAFFORESTATION
1/- St.Helena

HEAVY LIFT CRANE
1/6 St.Helena

LADY FIELD CHILDREN'S HOME
2/6 St.Helena

AGRICULTURAL TRAINING
5/- St.Helena

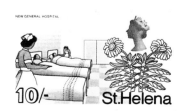

NEW GENERAL HOSPITAL
10/- St.Helena

LIFEBOAT JOHN DUTTON
£1 St.Helena

PLATE XXXIX

  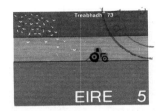 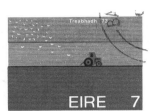

PLATE XL

PLATE XLI

PLATE XLII

BIBLIOGRAPHY

ALTMAN, Dennis. *Paper Ambassadors. The Politics of Stamps*, Angus and Roberston, Australia, 1991.

BARRETT, Dawn. *Design and Photography in Dutch Stamps*, V & K Publishing, The Netherlands, 1994.

BUFFIER, Dominique & JULLIEN, Pierre. *Les Plus Belles Histoires de Timbres*, Le Monde-Editions, Paris, 1992.

DIGGELMANN, Walter & SCHUNK, Volker. 'Markenkünstler - das halbe Lebeswerk', *Karl Bickel*, Buchsdruck und Verlag, 1986, pp35-53.

FINLAY, William. *An Illustrated History of Stamp Design*, Peter Lowe, London, 1974.

FORDE, Gerard. *Design in the Public Service. The Dutch PTT 1920-1990*, The Design Museum, London, 1990.

GENTLEMAN, David. *Design in Miniature*, Studio Vista, London, 1972.

GILIBERT, Marise. *Les Droits de l'homme et la philatélie*, Amnesty International, Paris, 1991.

GHIDELLI, Enrico. *Kunst im kleinen. Hans Erni als Gestalter von Brief marken un Medaillen*, 1995.

HAAREN, Hein van. 'Message Carriers. Dutch Postage Stamps', *Delta*, Autumn 1972, pp33-48.

HARTMANN, Fanny Hans Hartmann. *Ein Leben für die Grafik*, Stämpfli, Bern, 1993.

HEFTING, Paul. *Nederlandse Postzegels, 1987*, Staatsbedrijf der PTT en der SDU Uitgeverij, The Hague, 1988.

KHRIPOUNOFF, Alexis. 'Un parcours parmi les timbres, des origines à nos jours', *Russie-URSS 1914-1991. Changements de regards*, Musée d'Histoire contemporaine/BDIC, Paris, 1991, pp248-54.

LAURITZEN, Frederick. 'Propaganda Art in the Postage Stamps of the Third Reich', *The Journal of Decorative and Propaganda Arts*, Fall 1988, pp62-79.

MACKAY, James A. *Commonwealth Stamp Design 1840-1965*, British Museum, London, 1965.

MACKAY, James A. *Eire, the Story of Eire and her Stamps*, Philatelic Publishers, London, 1968.

MAURY, Arthur. *Histoire des timbres-poste*, Musée postale, Paris, 1907.

MOOR, Christiaan de. *Child Welfare Stamps in the Netherlands*, Netherlands Postal and Telecommunications Service, The Hague, 1969.

MURRAY-ROBINSON, Anne. 'Les timbres', *Grasset. Pionnier de l'Art nouveau*, Editions 24 heures, Lausanne, 1981, pp83-5.

PPT des Pays-Bas. *Les Timbres-poste des Pats-bas de 1929 à 1939*, Publications of the Dutch Post Office, The Hague, 1939.

ROSE, Stuart. *Royal Mail Stamp Design. A Survey of British Stamp Design*, Phaidon, London, 1980.

SCHATTSCHNEIDER, Doris. *Visions of Symmetry; notebooks, periodic drawings and related works of MC Escher*, Freeman, New York, 1990.

SCOTT, David. 'Posting Messages: the art and semiotics of the Irish Stamp' *Irish Arts Review Yearbook*, 1990, pp188-96.

SCOTT, David. 'Robert Ballagh and Contemporary Irish Stamp Design', *Irish Stamp News*, II no 1, 1991, pp20-25.

SCOTT, David. 'National Icons; the Semiotics of the French Stamp', *French Cultural Studies*, III, 1992, pp215-33.

SCOTT, David. 'The Art of Design; the postage stamps of Michael and Sylvia Goaman', *Gibbons Stamp Monthly*, September 1992, pp30-33.

SCOTT, David and HOEK, Leo. 'Une révolution en miniature. Sémiotique du timbre-poste commemoratif du Bicentenaire de la Révolution française', *Word & Image*, XI no 2, 1993, pp97-113.

SCOTT, David. 'Philately and the avant-garde; Dutch postage stamp design from the 1920s to the 1940s', *The Journal of Decorative and Propaganda Arts*, 20, 1994, pp58-77.

SCOTT, David. 'Rhétorique et image typographique; l'exemple du timbre-poste hollandais des années 50 aux années 90', *Rhétorique et image. Hommage à A Kibédi Varga*, Amsterdam, Rodopi, 1995, pp51-64.

SCOTT, David. 'Semiotics and Ideology in Mixed messages: the postage stamp', *Interactions* II, forthcoming, 1995.

TAVEL, Hans Christophe von. 'La Monnaie et les timbres', *L'Iconographie nationale, Ars Helvetica X , Arts et culture visuels en Suisse*, Editions Desertina, Disentis, Bern, 1992, pp170-87.

WHITE, Colin. *Edmund Dulac*, Studio Vista, London, 1976.

INDEX OF STAMP DESIGNERS

Note: this Index lists the names of the stamp designers whose work is illustrated in this book. It also includes names of artists or photographers associated with stamp design whose work is illustrated. Reference is by chapter numbers (bold print) followed by figure and/or plate numbers (bold roman numerals).